# TEN THINGS THEY DIDN'T TELL ME ABOUT LEADERSHIP

ALBERTO BELLO

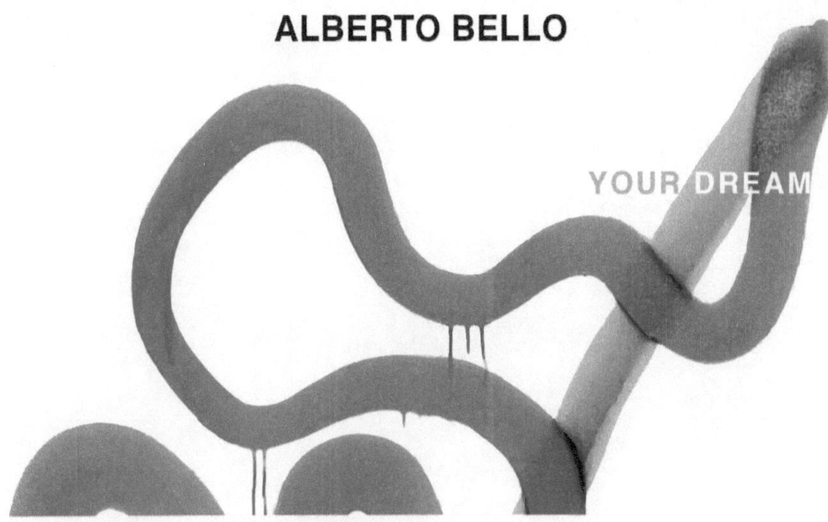


# TEN THINGS THEY DIDN'T TELL ME ABOUT LEADERSHIP

Hardcover ISBN: 979-8-8229-5819-7
Paperback ISBN: 979-8-8229-5820-3

# ADVANCE PRAISE

In his prophetic book "***Ten Things They Didn't Tell Me About Leadership***"; Pastor Alberto Bello's words captivate the heart and mind quickly.

His words leap from the page with a cadence akin to a fiery sermon couched in practical insights and wisdom to help answer perplexing issues facing modern leaders in the church and the world today. This is not a how-to guide, but this is a manifesto about personal preparation needed for the process and burden of leadership.

Pastor Alberto Bello weaves a powerful tapestry of his own personal leadership journey with leaders found in the bible, that takes the reader into deeper reflection of their own leadership effectiveness.

I highly recommend this powerful work to churches, businesses, the community, families and individuals. Get ready to be inspired and transformed in your leadership call to duty! You will be blessed, challenged and encouraged to soar to new heights as you look to the Creator of leadership, our Lord and Savior Jesus Christ.

*—Ron Brown,*
*Executive Director and CEO of Teen*
*Challenge of Southern California*

"Alberto Bello has written the manifesto for leaders who have faced the challenges and hardships of the ministry life. Throughout these pages he shares with authenticity the struggles and setbacks that he has faced, while laying out a blueprint on how to overcome these obstacles that any and all leaders will face. He reminds us that a leader is not measured by how many times they are knocked down but by how many times they get up and face the giant before them. I HIGHLY recommend you and your team read this inspiring work from my friend. You will not be disappointed."

**—Chris Sonksen**
*Author/Pastor/Coach*

"Ten Things They Didn't Tell Me About Leadership" bridges the gap between theory and practice. A must read for anyone wanting to understand the connection between our daily lives and the spiritual leadership principles needed to succeed. No matter if it's through friendships, marriage, parenting, work life, etc... Alberto Bello has an incredible gift of using relatable experiences to help others in their self development journey.

**—Kyle Shiloh**
*CEO, Gameday Sports Academy*

"This book evokes deep feelings and nostalgia, bringing tenderness to a painful season in my life. Pastor Alberto excels at connecting with readers by sharing his personal experiences and anecdotes, then guiding them toward the right perspective on it all.

Alberto also touches on powerful points and conclusions that could only come from God's revelation and firsthand experience. His insights, shaped by adversity and seeming failures, offer a fresh perspective that helps us enjoy the journey and feel assured of aligning with God's purposes for our lives.

I also appreciate how Alberto exposes the enemy's tactics to derail us from our calling. To any pastor or leader who has faced discouragement or felt the sting of failure, I highly recommend this book. It not only offers valuable life lessons from Alberto's experiences and powerful biblical principles every Christian should learn but also practical applications.

As someone who considers Alberto a dear friend, I can attest to his heart for the church and ministry leaders. He truly embodies a pastor's heart."

**—Elias Recinos,**
*Pastor at City On A Hill*

# DEDICATION

I dedicate this book to my wife, Ashley, whose unwavering support has been the solid foundation on which this book was built. This book wouldn't exist without her unwavering belief in me and encouragement to write it. She truly deserves the credit because I was never alone; she was always by my side. Ashley's support and love have been the driving force behind this book, and I am grateful for her unwavering patience and understanding as I poured my heart and soul into its creation. Her insights and perspectives have added depth and richness to the pages, making this book truly collaborative.

Ashley, your unwavering support has been the foundation on which this book was built, and I am eternally grateful for your love and encouragement. You truly deserve the credit because I was never alone on this journey; you were always by my side.

# CONTENTS

# INTRODUCTION

Have you ever felt alone on your leadership journey? Maybe you've felt like no one understands what you're going through or has had the right words to say amid your leadership crisis.

If that's you, I want you to know that you've picked the right book to read. This book is not about developing ideal growth systems or solid strategies for your church or organization that will increase productivity.

This book is about you! It's about your journey behind the scenes. It's about dealing with matters of the heart, filling the deficits in your character, and unveiling the leadership talks I wish someone had had with me.

This book is not just about spiritual leadership principles but practical ones that I have learned the hard way. The application is not just simple but empowering; the experiences are relatable and can guide you. This book is not just for those on the fringes of quitting but for those who have failed, reminding them that they're in good company. All great leaders have failed repeatedly. It's not about how many times you fall but how many times you get back up.

My leadership journey was not a straight shot to the top. I had a completely different picture in my mind of what my journey would look like. To my surprise, it looked nothing like I thought it would. I was under the impression that I would shoot to the top of my dreams and God's vision for my life. I knew it would be a journey of ups and downs, twists and turns, setbacks and comebacks.

At that moment, I could never understand what God was doing, but now, looking back, I can see His hand was all over me and my journey. I made many mistakes and encountered setbacks, but in the end, they made me the leader I am today. I still have a long way to go, but I must acknowledge where I once was.

This book inspires and encourages you wherever you are on the leadership journey. Whether you're in a leadership position at church or a business or have a business, I believe this book will speak to you right where you are.

I always longed for someone who understood my process while going through different seasons but finding that person took a lot of work. You may feel alone in your journey; if that's you, I want this book to make you feel like you're not alone. You're not just seen but understood and valued more than you know.

You've got this! I pray that God will speak to you mightily and profoundly, filling you with inspiration and hope!

**1**

# WHO ARE YOU?

*The value of identity, of course, is so often with it comes purpose.*
–Richard Grant

*Be yourself; everyone else is already taken.*
–Oscar Wilde

remember ninth grade like it was yesterday. This was the beginning of high school. I was no longer just a junior high kid; I was now a man. Okay...Well... That's going a bit far, but that's how I felt then. I have to be honest and say that I was looking for a girlfriend a whole lot more than I was looking to pass my science class. I was absolutely girl crazy.

I'll never forget the day I saw "the one." Yup, the one! The one that I wanted to date. When I first saw her, the heavens opened up, the angels appeared, and they began to sing, "This is the one." We know that didn't happen, but this hopped-up-on-testosterone teen was sure she was the one.

Back then, there wasn't social media, so we couldn't go to someone's Instagram or Facebook page and learn all there was to know about them. I was old school and had to stalk...I mean, follow her, to figure out who she was and her name.

Well, I found out her name was Rosa, and Rosa was a junior. I was not only in love, but I was in love with an older woman. I did everything I could to get Rosa to notice me, but to no avail.

I have to be honest; I was frustrated and felt like a failure. I was perplexed why Rosa wouldn't give me the time of day. Maybe it was because I was a freshman, but I digress. After the frustration had settled, I went to her best friend and asked her why Rosa would ignore me. She told me that Rosa didn't like my style. She had liked guys who dressed a certain way, had a particular haircut, and had a different style.

This was my "aha" moment because all I had to do was change everything about me in twenty-four hours so that she would notice me. After this, I knew that I needed to change my wardrobe, so I went to my dad and asked him if he could take me shopping, and he did. He did what any Hispanic father would: do he took me to the swap meet. It didn't stop there; I even went to the barber and got a new haircut. I was confident that this was going to work.

I have some news for you, ladies and gentlemen: It worked. That very next week, Rosa noticed me, and we exchanged beeper numbers and began to talk on the phone. I mean, this relationship was going places. I remember about three weeks into our relationship, we took a trip to Magic Mountain, a theme park in Southern California. It was a serious relationship in high school if you went on a date with a girl to Magic Mountain.

Things were going well at Magic Mountain until they weren't. We had been at the park for most of the day, but I noticed that Rosa was acting funny, and at the time, I had no idea why. We began to approach the Batman ride, and that's when things took a turn for the worse. She broke up with me. She could have waited until Revolution, the ride, but nope. She left me there, standing alone. Honestly, it sucked.

I found myself standing in front of the Batman ride in weird clothes, a weirder haircut, and a style that wasn't even my own. It was at that moment that I realized that I was trying to be something I was never created to be, to have something I was never created to have.

For me, this hard truth is often what most of us genuinely wrestle with. So many of us are trying to be something that God never created us to be in order to have something that He didn't

SO  MANY  OF  US
ARE  TRYING TO  BE
SOMETHING  THAT
GOD  NEVER
CREATED  US  TO BE

WHO ARE YOU?

IN ORDER TO HAVE
SOMETHING THAT
HE DIDN'T MAKE US
TO HAVE.

make us to have. It's so easy to get lost in the labels thrown at us from this world, social media, friends, and even family. Sometimes, it's hard to honestly know who you are because everyone has ideas about who you should be and what you should do.

> **So many of us are trying to be something that God never created us to be in order to have something that He didn't make us to have.**

I look at David's life as he's on his way to fight Goliath (I Samuel 17). This was a pivotal moment for David. This would be the moment that shifted the trajectory of his life. This would be the moment that would begin his journey to be king outside of his king-anointing party that he previously had.

## Identity Crisis in the Making

The giant, Goliath, had been tormenting the people of Israel for some time and causing fear among the people. This was a remarkable moment because no one in the land would dare approach Goliath—none but David. King Saul sanctioned this moment, and David got ready to fight Goliath. He only knew how to do it with a slingshot and a few rocks. As he walked past the king, the king didn't think this kid could do it—at least not with what he was wearing or carrying.

At this moment, the king attempted to place his armor on David, and he succeeded. David took on the armor, but the only problem with this is that the king's armor was made to fit only the king and the king alone. Saul was tall, and David wasn't. This armor was contoured for Saul and would never fit David.

So why did David take on the armor? Scripture isn't clear on this, but maybe he took on Saul's armor because he felt the weight and pressure of the people watching him, he felt the pressure of his leader, and perhaps he felt insecure after the suggestion to take on the armor came about.

David was a skilled fighter, fighting off lions, tigers, and bears— oh me, oh my! He had been fighting off wild beasts in green pastures all his life while tending his sheep. David spent time writing Psalms, speaking to God, praising God, and being in a relationship with Him. If anything, David knew who he was, but maybe he didn't know who he wasn't.

David put on the armor and took a step in the right direction while wearing the wrong layers. The Bible indicates that he took a step in "vain," meaning that his step was wasted. Yes, David was going the right way, but he wasn't in his skin. He wasn't going to fight in the way God had fashioned him to for this moment. So what did David do?

Well, he took the armor off after taking that step in vain. I want to know what David was thinking when he took that step. Was he thinking, "This isn't me?" Was he asking himself, "Why am I doing this when I know how to fight?" Scripture doesn't indicate, but I can only imagine some things going through his mind.

When he finally came to his senses, he threw off the armor and ran into his God-given destiny in the way he knew how. It was him being himself, confident in who his God was and who his God had created him to be. He would have had a different result if he had kept the armor on.

## Knowing Who You Are

This story often describes us. We feel like we have to be someone or something we're not to obtain something that was already ours. One of the most incredible things we can do as followers of Jesus is to know who we are and who we aren't.

We need to walk with greater confidence, authority, and acceptance. We must comprehend that when we come into the family of faith and a relationship with Jesus, we begin as children of God; we become sons or daughters. This is very key to know, hold, and walk in.

Before Jesus was launched into the fullness of His ministry journey here on earth, He had a defining moment at the Jordan River. John the Baptist baptized him, and as He came out of the water, there was a unique and defining moment. The heavens were open, and you had God the Father, Son, and Holy Spirit all present in the same space for the first time in the New Testament, and God spoke. What did He say? He said, "This is my Son whom I love and am well pleased with" (Matthew 3:17).

After this moment, Jesus was launched into the wilderness for forty days and then into His earthly ministry assignment. Even the Son of God had to be affirmed in this moment that He was a son and had to know that God was pleased with His being, not just His doing. An identity-marking moment set the stage for the rest of Jesus's' life on earth.

Before Jesus was a savior, He was a son.

We need to understand that deeply today—that you're a child of God, whether a son or a daughter. Let me save you years of searching and seeking to find who you are and a ton of money in therapy. You're a child of God, and He is pleased with you and loves you.

You also have to be on guard because the devil has a plan to get you to doubt your identity in God. He can limit your walking in authority if he can get you to doubt your identity. You might be asking, "what does that mean?" After Jesus was baptized and had this defining moment of identity marking, the Holy Spirit led him into the wilderness to be tested for forty days and forty nights.

During that time, the devil came to Jesus in an attempt to lead Jesus to fall into temptation and forfeit His place on earth. The devil tried to get Jesus to doubt His identity so that He could corner Him into compromising His mission. The devil said to Jesus, "If you are the Son of God, tell these stones to become bread." He once again said to Jesus, "If you are the Son of God, throw yourself down. For it is written: 'He will command his angels concerning you, and they will lift you up in their hands so that you will not strike your foot against a stone.'"

The devil's whole ploy was to get Jesus to doubt what God spoke over Him so that He would fall into sin, just like he did to Adam and Eve in the Garden of Eden. Obviously, Jesus didn't succumb to the devil's tactics, and He came back at Him with scripture. Eventually, the devil left Jesus.

How important is it for you to know your place in God's family? Extremely important. If the first thing that the devil attempted to do was get Jesus to doubt His identity and place right after He was affirmed, what do you think he'll try to do to you? One moment, the voice of heaven declares, "This is my son," and in another moment, the deceiver's voice probes Jesus with the words of doubt, trying to diminish his deity and place.

Why is the devil so bent on you not fully knowing who you are? Why is he so proactive in his attempts to get you to believe that you're a spiritual orphan? Because he knows that the minute you know who God truly is in your life and He reveals who you truly are, unprecedented power will follow you and lead you to victory and authority. Spiritual authority is a byproduct of identity.

## Spiritual Authority is a Byproduct of Identity

I spent much of my ministry life up to this point on a journey to discover who I was. I found my validation and identity in my doing rather than my being. My whole personhood was wrapped up in my accomplishments, accolades, the conferences I spoke at, the TV show I once had, and the people I worked for. I was caught up in the trap that the enemy set before me. I lost myself, not in the way Jesus calls us to, but in the worst way possible.

I took on the armor of what others wanted me to be or needed me to be so that I could find some sense of acceptance. In the process, God had to allow some significant crushing to come to rid me of myself so that I could be filled with His acceptance. In hindsight, I'm grateful for the crushing because it produced the better version of myself and the better leader in me. Knowing who I am and who I'm not has been an essential part of me being able to lead and love at the level that I do. It's given me a greater confidence, not in myself, but in the God who dwells in me.

## Knowing Your Authority

The most dangerous type of Christian and Christian leader is the one who knows their God-given authority and walks entirely in it. When Paul implores us in Ephesians chapter six to put on the

THE MOST DANGER-
OUS TYPE OF
CHRISTIAN AND
CHRISTIAN LEADER IS
THE ONE WHO KNOWS
THEIR GOD-GIVEN
AUTHORITY AND WALKS
ENTIRELY IN IT.

WHO ARE YOU?

whole armor of God and stand firm, he's referencing the armor of a Roman soldier. Why would Paul use such a secular reference when driving in a point to deliver? It's simple, because a Roman soldier would stand tall, proud, firm, and confident. Why is that? Because a Roman soldier knew who they represented. A Roman soldier knew who stood behind them, who marched alongside them, and who went before them—the Roman authority.

Paul is trying to drive to the point that we, as believers in Jesus, should be able to walk with such authority and confidence because we know who is behind us, who lives in us, and who goes before us. The King of Kings and the Lord of Lords! He is the beginning and the end, and He occupies all within that space. This should give you the confidence that you need to lead a life of victory and lead others well.

With this knowledge, why are so many believers walking around like spiritual orphans? We don't know what being a child of God means.

In a nutshell, it means you're accepted. Maybe no one else has ever accepted you for who you are, with your quirks and all, but the Father does. This is where you find your true identity. If you don't get this now, you'll always work for acceptance or from a place of acceptance.

## Acceptance Is Key

With that acceptance, you must also accept your flaws and weaknesses just as much as your strong points and gifting. So many leaders spend so much time trying to mask their deficiencies to cover up what everyone already knows. It's in the weakened areas of our lives where God truly gets the glory and what He tends to use the most. In 2 Corinthians 12, Paul writes, "My grace is sufficient for you, for my power is made perfect in weakness." Therefore, I will boast all the more gladly about my weaknesses so that Christ's power may rest on me." What in the world are you saying, Paul? This scripture feels so contrary to how we live.

Paul tells us that if he brags, posts, shares, or declares anything, it will be his weakness because that's where he has to depend on God the most, and God gets all the credit. We've flipped the script in today's culture, making it seem that we have to portray that all is well and that we've got it all together. We all have weaknesses, and we must learn to embrace them and accept them as God does.

Whenever I get up on the platform to speak at church, a conference, or a meeting, I'm as nervous as all outdoors. Most people think that public speaking comes naturally to me, and maybe it does, but it sure doesn't feel that way. My nerves get the best of me, I doubt my ability to preach and I'm often freaking out on the inside more than I'm showing it. Although this tends to be my reality, it's the very thing that God uses to get me to depend on Him wholeheartedly. It's also the thing that He gets the most glory in because without the Holy Spirit, my words would fall flat, and I would probably never set foot on a stage again. I've learned to accept my weakness as part of my uniqueness.

Whenever I go on the platform to preach, I tell myself three things that have helped me tremendously. I say the following:

1. You have nothing to prove to God.
2. You have nothing to prove to these people.
3. You have nothing to prove to yourself.

## It All Comes Together

I love what the Apostle Paul says in Ephesians 1:1. He declares the following with much confidence, not arrogance. "Paul, an apostle of Christ Jesus by the will of God, To God's holy people in Ephesus, the faithful in Christ Jesus:" Paul declared four profound principles in this verse. He stated who he was, what he was called to do, who he did it for, and where his authority came from.

This is who I am, I'm Paul.

This is what I do; I'm an Apostle.

This is who I do it for: God's people in Ephesus.

This is where my authority comes from God alone.

My questions to you would be, "Who are you?" "What have you been called to do?" "Who are you doing it for?" "Where does your authority come from?"

Don't get so caught up in your doing that you forget about your being—being a child of God. If you live from that and lead from that place, everything else will fall into place.

There's nothing worse than getting thrown into the fullness of God's assignment for you when you're not even sure who you are. That is nothing more than a recipe for disaster. What the world doesn't need is another carbon copy of a leader. We need authentic leaders. We need you to be you.

You have to know who you are and who you aren't. What armor do you have to strip off today? What labels have you allowed to be placed on you that you've been carrying your entire life and need to be stripped away? What have you taken on just to be accepted into particular circles, streams, and places that need to go?

You'll only reach your fullest potential once you take care of this one thing. Take it from me, you belong to God and he accepts you. Walk in confidence and walk victoriously. Today is the day!

**Reflection Questions:**

1. Have I been walking in my God-given authority and acceptance, or have I found my identity and acceptance in what I
   do and from the people I do it with?
2. What steps can I take today to be assured that I belong to God
   and have the authority to lead myself and others?
3. What is God calling me to do in this season of my life for
   which He's given the grace, and how do I get there?

# THE COMPARISON TRAP

*Comparison is the thief of joy.*
–Theodore Roosevelt

*Don't compare your life to others. There's no comparison between the sun and the moon. They shine when it's their time.*
–Unknown

'm from Los Angeles, so that means that I'm an aggressive driver by nature. If you wanted to survive the mean streets out there, you had to be. Before becoming a pastor, I had high hopes for becoming a rapper, if you couldn't tell. Anyway, have you ever been driving along the freeway, parkway, or whatever you call it, and you're having a good day because there's no traffic? You're in your lane, you have your favorite worship song on, and you're belting out the lyrics as though you lead worship on Sundays from the stage. You're feeling good because you might get to your destination early with enough time to grab a coffee and still make your appointment with a few minutes to spare. And then...

All of a sudden, your lane begins to slow down. You're trying to keep it cool, telling yourself that it will speed up again, but your lane is now at a dead stop. So what do you do? You start looking to your right and left and notice that every lane is moving but yours. So what do you do when that happens? If you're like me, you would swerve into the moving lane, hoping to advance. The problem is that the minute you do that, without fail, that lane comes to a complete stop, and the lane that you were in begins to move.

The frustration builds, and you no longer listen to worship music. Instead, you've switched the music to some Tupac or Biggie Smalls because you feel slightly "gangsta." So you're now on a mission to get back into your lane, but you can't use your signal because the person next to you won't let you in, and now you're going to a new level by marking cars, which means that you've used a particular car as a marker to help you determine what lane you should stay in. You spend the entire time going from lane to lane, trying to find the fastest one to get you to your destination. When you finally reach the exit, you notice the car you used as a marker is several cars ahead of you, and you realize that if you had just stayed in your lane, you would have gotten to your exit in the time you needed to. Your neck got you in trouble, so you kept looking to the right and the left and comparing your lane and progress to the other lanes around you.

We all struggle with comparison, and it's not always in a healthy way. Last time I checked, comparison wasn't part of the fruit of the spirit, yet we embody it as if it were. Comparison can be good if it's helping positively fuel your mission and learning from those who are ahead of you, but most times, that isn't the case.

> ## We all struggle with comparison, and it's not always in a healthy way.

Comparison does a few things. It can breed feelings of superiority or inferiority. This means that comparison will either make you feel better about someone else's progress or leave you feeling less than because of someone else's progress; neither of those is a good thing. Superiority is prideful in itself, the fact that you're using someone else's lack of progress to fuel your insecurity and emotional complexity indicates that something is off.

The feeling of superiority can also close your eyes to recognizing where you're at along your journey because you often compare yourself to someone miles behind you as it pertains to progress and gives you a sense of false gratification. You should be further along the process, but looking to those not on your level might hold you back from actual progress. Feelings of superiority are a breeding ground for pride and arrogance, and pride is like bad breath; everyone knows you have it, except for you. It usually puffs you up so your head can't fit through the door.

Comparison can also make you feel less than others. It can cause you to look at someone who seems to have more success than you in your specialty, whether pastoring, being a business owner, parenting, or even financially. When you compare yourself to someone who is ahead of you and allow it to bring you down, it can be debilitating. It can cause you to feel like a failure, it can get you to become frustrated with God and your process, and it can take your eyes off the beauty that is all around you and even make you bitter. It turns you into a "hater!" By that, I mean you dislike everything and everyone that threatens your success or prevents you from getting the attention of others

That's why genuinely celebrating people and their progress is so challenging. It's because our insecurity and bitterness don't allow us to. Sometimes, it seems like pastors are the worst at this. We struggle to celebrate and champion each other because of deep insecurity. Proximity also plays into this. It's easy to acknowledge someone and be happy for them when they're far from you because they pose no threat, but they become your enemy when they're down the street from you.

The Apostle Paul was a confident guy. He understood what it meant to stay in his lane. Let's take a look at what he said:

PRIDE IS LIKE BAD BREATH:

# EVERYONE KNOWS YOU HAVE IT, EXCEPT FOR YOU.

*"We will not boast about things done outside our area of authority.
We will boast only about what has happened within the boundaries
of the work God has given us, which includes our working with you."*
(2 Corinthians 10:13, NLT)

Paul said that he would only focus on what was before him and directly in his lane and that if he were going to be braggadocios about anything, it would be about what was going on within the parameters God had given him.

This is precisely how we should live our lives—staying focused on what's before us and what's in our lane. We must spend less time comparing ourselves to others when it's only led us to dark places. We all have done it, and we all do it. It's easier said than done. When you first meet someone, you typically size them up, from their outfit to their style and family, and even look at the car they drive. We usually use this gauge to determine whether you want to have someone in your circle.

Many of you will never go beyond where you're at because you surround yourself with people beneath you so that you always feel ahead. Many of your staff, teams, churches, and businesses are that way because you have to be the smartest in the room. You have to be the savior of the organization. That's toxic thinking and toxic living.

> **Many of you will never go beyond whereyou're at because you surround yourself with people beneath you so thatyou always feel ahead.**

## Why do We Compare Ourselves?

Comparison is a byproduct of insecurity and disappointment. These are the two times we find ourselves the most vulnerable and susceptible to comparing ourselves to others. It's usually during these moments that we become "scrolling monsters." There's nothing unhealthier than grabbing our phones and jumping onto Instagram or Facebook to see what others are doing and how things are playing out for them when we're at a low. We know it's not the wisest decision, but we all make it ourselves. Why do we subject ourselves to that kind of torture? Because it helps us build our case of frustration, resentment, and anger.

I remember being a church planter in Hollywood and having back-to-back Sundays after we launched with only thirty-something people. Every weekend seemed like an additional nail into my hyperbole pastoral coffin. Weekend after weekend, we stayed at this number. Let's note that we were meeting on the campus of an elementary school inside the Michael Jackson Auditorium. Thirty people inside a school auditorium is depressing in itself; now, imagine every week.

The days that we would get the most significant number of visitors was when the Hollywood Tour Bus would stop in front of the school and allow all foreign tourists to get off and come inside for a tour. Michael Jackson attended the school when he was a child. Other than that, it felt like I was drowning in my misery and disappointment. A disappointment can be defined as a misplaced expectation, and I, for one, had misplaced all of my expectations on what I thought the process and progress were going to look like for me.

To make matters worse, and for some odd reason, I would scroll through social media on Sundays after church only to see other church planters have record attendance at their services. I knew it wasn't healthy, but I did it to myself anyway. Great churches with big-name pastors surrounded us, and I was a little fish in a massive pond.

One Sunday, one of the newer church plants in Hollywood rented the nightclub across the street from us, and we had the exact service times. I could stand out front and watch a line of cars park on our street, but they only parked there to attend the other church. People would get out of their cars confused, looking for the other church, but seeing our signs, I would just point them to the nightclub because I knew where they were going. It wasn't to our place, that's for sure.

## I Didn't Like My Lane

This entire season of defeat caused me to feel like I wasn't worthy. It caused me to feel like maybe God wasn't in it. It caused me to feel like I wasn't a good leader, and eventually, I walked into that. That was also the fuel I used to drive myself to an unhealthy pace and places. The building of the Kingdom didn't drive me; I was driven by building my wounded ego. I forgot to realize that we're all in different seasons and places. We each have a lane that God has us on, and we each have a measure of grace to run in that lane. The problem was that I didn't like my lane. I didn't think that trying to merge lanes would be a bad thing, but in the end, it was just me running from what God was attempting to do in me so that He could do something profound through me.

God is more concerned with who you are becoming along the journey versus getting you to the destination. Often, we idolize the vision to an unhealthy extent, forgetting about the process in between.

GOD IS MORE
CONCERNED WITH
WHO YOU
ARE
BECOMING
ALONG
THE JOURNEY
VERSUS GETTING
TO YOUR
DESTINATION

If we could be honest for just a minute, that would imply that I've been lying the entire book…just kidding. We all have insecurities that must be kept at bay. This means that all of us will have to deal with our insecurities in some way, shape, or form because we all have them; the real question is, "How are we dealing with those insecurities?" The truth is that most people don't healthily deal with them. Instead, they cope with unhealthy coping mechanisms such as walking in bitterness, resentment, anger, frustration, and even becoming the thing that they despise the most, which is a "hater." Yes, I said it, a "hater.". Every leader has insecurities; sometimes, God calls the most insecure people to lead. Just look at the biblical characters that God called Moises, Gideon, Jeremiah, and Peter, and the list could go on and on. That could be because He wants to use those who will rely not on their strength but upon Him. He did choose the foolish things of this world to confound the wise, and I have to admit that I'm one of those foolish things.

## ▍ "And all God's people said, amen!"

The difference between a good leader and a great leader is that great leaders learn to manage their insecurities and keep them at bay versus attempting to bury them and pretend that they don't exist. They learn to manage those negative and toxic emotions through healthy means and essentially die to those insecurities for the greater good of their personal, mental, and spiritual health and the health of those they lead.

Disappointment is a nesting ground for comparison. It can leave you feeling betrayed by God and by others. If you're not careful, disappointment can cause other toxic emotions to spring up and have their way with your mind. The best thing to do is to learn how to manage your expectations better and be prepared so that if things don't go according to plan, you'll stay firm and confident in what God is doing in you and through you.

Sometimes, disappointment is the very mechanism God will use to offend the mind so that He can expose the heart, which means He'll allow disappointment to come to show you where you are in your maturity. It might mean He has some things that He wants to see tweaked in you before He moves you forward into success. Disappointment, when not managed correctly, will cause you to look over the fence at others who seem to be living on the greener grass and get you to believe that you're not able, you're not worthy, and you're less than others; all of which are not true.

> **Sometimes, disappointment is the very mechanism God will use to offend the mind so that He can expose the heart, which means He'll allow disappointment to come to show you where you are in your maturity.**

## Overcoming the Comparison Trap (Honor, Contentment, and Joy)

The question is, how do we overcome the feelings of comparison in our lives? How can we die in this specific area of our hearts? Well, you combat the adverse side effects of comparison by learning the art of honoring others. Honoring those around you is a great way to kill pride and insecurity within us.

What would it look like if you encouraged someone in your industry far ahead of you with a kind email, note, or text? What would it look like if you hit the "like" button on that Instagram post and left a comment instead of trolling around? What if, at the next staff meeting, you acknowledge someone in the room who's better than you in a particular area and encourage them in front of your staff? You'd look like a natural leader, that's for sure. These small acts will go a long way. Honor can put those fleshly desires to death and give us the peace to stay focused on our lane and content.

Content does not mean complacent. It just means you're satisfied with where God has you, but you'll still press on to reach your dreams, goals, and vision. The Apostle Paul gives us some insight into this idea of contentment. This guy didn't stay still but always kept going on to plant churches and encourage the body, and he even wrote a majority of the New Testament.

"I am not saying this because I am in need, for I have learned to be content, whatever the circumstances. I know what it is to be in need and what it is to have plenty. I have learned the secret of being content in any and every situation, whether well-fed or hungry, whether living in plenty or want. I can do all this through him who gives me strength." (Philippians 4:11-13, NIV) Essentially, Paul was saying that no matter the season, the situation, or the circumstance, he had learned the secret to being content. In this context, it meant that as long as he had Jesus in his life, he was good to go—that Jesus was the one who sustained him in all circumstances.

You need to adopt that view of our lives and circumstances. No matter the season of our lives, ministry, or journey, as long as we have Jesus, we can walk in unprecedented joy and unshakable peace.

> **No matter the season of our lives, ministry, or journey, as long as we have Jesus; we can walk in unprecedented joy and unshakable peace.**

It would benefit you the most to learn how to enjoy the journey. People would ask me if there was anything I could have done differently in my past ministry experiences, what would that be? My response is always quick and straightforward. I told them I wished I would have enjoyed the journey. When you take your eyes off Jesus and put them on other lanes and over the fence to find greener grass, you rob yourself of the beauty around you. Joy does not imply perfection or a result of blessings; joy can find a reason for gladness in any season, no matter the cause or effect. Joy is for the spiritually mature who knows there is still a reason to find joy and draw strength from it, even on the most challenging days.

Be sure to carry that joy with you because it will quickly eradicate any bitterness, resentment, or disappointment in the results. In the end, you have one job: to be obedient to Christ. The rest is up to Him. You obey; He produces the harvest.

Today is the day you quit walking around defeated. Today may be the day you quit walking around feeling less than. Today is when you look to Jesus and thank Him for where you're at and where He's taking you; letting go of the planned process to allow His way to take precedence.

Remember, your journey is unique, just like the sun and the moon. They don't compare; they simply shine when it's their time. So, don't compare your life to others; embrace your lane and shine in your own time.

## Reflection Questions:

1. Where has comparison tripped you up, and how do you plan to get ahead of it?
2. What can you do in this season to show honor to someone around you who's in your same industry or area of ministry?
3. How will you overcome the feeling to compare when you're feeling disappointed and defeated?

# 3

# YOU'LL WANT TO GIVE UP

*Where the battle rages, there the loyalty of the soldier is proved.*
–Martin Luther

*The ragamuffin who sees his life as a voyage of discovery and runs the risk of failure has a better feel for faithfulness than the timid man who hides behind the law and never finds out who he is at all.*
–Brennan Manning, *The Ragamuffin Gospel*

During a recent lunch with a young and successful business owner and myself, he posed a thought-provoking question. His query shed light on the perspective of an outsider looking in on a successful endeavor. He asked, "What, in your opinion, has been the driving force behind your success as a new church?" This question, in essence, was a request for the secret to our success. The answer, as you might have guessed, was faithfulness.

I sat there with a dramatic pause because it's what I do. I smiled, then told him that the secret to our success has been one thing and one thing only: faithfulness. Most people today seek quick results and quick methods to have successful churches, ministries, businesses, and even marriages. It indicates that most people want to see an explosion of success right out of the jump before putting in the hard work over a long period. But true success, the kind that lasts, comes from being faithful, from persevering even when the results aren't immediate. There is no recipe for overnight success because 99.9 percent of people have never been overnight successes. I made that percentage up, but you get my point.

After my response, he looked at me confused because he imagined I would say that our worship, kid's ministry, or even my preaching had brought success. All those things are needed in a healthy and thriving church, but that wasn't the precipice for it. It was simply being faithful to what was in front of me. I learned to be faithful with the little in my hand. It was learning to be faithful with my talents and mine only.

Our journey was not without its share of failures. In fact, I can't even begin to count the number of times we stumbled before we found our footing. But each failure was a stepping stone, a testament to our endurance and faithfulness. It was as if our faithfulness was being stored in heaven, and God poured out His blessing at the right time. The failures, far from being setbacks, were integral parts of our journey, making our eventual success all the more rewarding.

## Endurance is Key

It would help if you learned the art of endurance and faithfulness to succeed at anything. God will often give you the vision and then lead you through the valley of humility to work it out. Just because He shows you the final product or the result does not indicate that you will obtain it at that moment or even in the next few moments. Reaching that vision or goal might take weeks, months, and years. But remember, every step you take, every moment of endurance, brings you closer to your goal. In Matthew 7:6, Jesus says, "Don't cast your pearls before swine. If you do, the pigs will trample the pearls with their little feet." This is a reminder to be patient and not rush the process, as the reward will be all the more satisfying when it comes.

Jesus used a powerful analogy to illustrate this point. He said, "Don't cast your pearls before swine. If you do, the pigs will trample the pearls with their little feet." In other words, giving something precious to someone who doesn't understand its value is a waste. God doesn't want to give you what you haven't worked for. The only way to truly appreciate the value of something is when you've had to invest in it with blood, sweat, and tears.

EACH FAILURE WAS A STEPPING STONE, A TESTAMENT TO OUR ENDURANCE &  FAITHFULNESS & IT MADE OUR EVENTUAL SUCCESS ALL THE MORE REWARDING

**The only way to understand the actual value of something is when you've had to invest in it with blood, sweat, and tears.**

I have four children, and my wife and I have repeatedly told our kids, "Do you guys think that money grows on trees?" I'm embarrassed to admit that because my dad used to take me to the backyard of our house and ask me the same question while pointing to our tree. I said I would never do that to my kid, and here we are. Anyway, back to the story. We tried everything to get them to see that what they had was enough or if they wanted something that we wouldn't just give them. This was a difficult concept for them to grasp, so I had an idea to help drive them to the point of learning the value of a dollar. I created a weekly chore chart for each child, even the four-year-old because she asked me to do it. It included a breakdown of daily chores and how much I would pay for each chore.

I've never seen my kids so excited to clean their rooms, do the dishes, and feed the dog. They began to see if they completed some work and got their hands a little dirty to earn money they could save and purchase the things they wanted. It was a game changer; I'm more broke than ever because money doesn't grow on trees, but it grows on me. The whole point is that I wanted my children to learn the value of things and to learn to take care of their things.

God is the same way with us. Imagine if He just gave us everything we asked for and wanted in the moment. We wouldn't know how to handle it, and we would ruin something created to be a good thing but at the right time, His time.

## Know Your Season

This is why I believe that God takes us through challenging seasons along the path toward success. He does some of His most extraordinary work in those seasons if we're willing to submit to the process. When you think about the seasons we go through, there's winter, spring, summer, and fall. Now I live in Bakersfield, California, so that means we get hot and hotter. Each season serves a purpose, and with each season, we're required to change and adjust to match the season that we're in.

For example, summertime can be sweltering, so we tend to dress differently than in the winter. We've begun to remove layers of clothes to match the season. Very rarely do you see someone wearing a turtleneck and a coat in the summer; that would be ridiculous. Instead, you see people in t-shirts, shorts, and flip-flops. In the winter, though, you add layers of clothing due to the cold weather. People are no longer wearing just T-shirts, flip-flops, and shorts. Instead, they're adding layers of clothing to stay warm. Why? Because each season must bring about a change.

It's the same with our spiritual season along the journey. Sometimes, God brings certain seasons because there are things that He wants to remove from your heart, character, or life, and then there are other seasons in which He's attempting to add things to you. The list can go on and on, such as patience, wisdom, and Godly character. Each season brings a purpose that will help you succeed in the future. God is more concerned about building a solid infrastructure to sustain the weight of the blessing that He will bring you. If we are not careful and try to speed up specific processes or take shortcuts, the blessing created to bless you might crush you instead.

IF WE ARE NOT CAREFUL AND TRY TO SPEED UP SPECIFIC PROCESSES OR TAKE SHORTCUTS, THE BLESSING CREATED TO BLESS YOU MIGHT

# CRUSH YOU INSTEAD

Here is the promise you can take to the bank regarding each season. God is the Good Shepherd who walks with you through each season of your life and leadership process. David said it best in Psalm 23 when he talks about walking alongside the still waters, the green pastures, and through the valley of the shadow of death. He's referring to different seasons that he's had to walk through. The incredible part of all of that is at the beginning of the Psalm, he begins with "The Lord is my Shepherd."

What does that even imply? Jesus, in John 14, gives overarching characteristics of a shepherd as He references Himself as the Good Shepherd. A good shepherd would be one who would always be near to his sheep, would always guide his sheep, and would always protect his sheep no matter the cost. Jesus is reminding you today that He is the Good Shepherd who is guiding you through every season; He's near to you in every season, even if you can't sense it, and He's going to protect you in every season.

That doesn't mean that you won't experience turbulence or bumps and bruises along the way. It means that He will protect your inheritance in heaven and that your name will be etched into the Lamb's Book of Life. It means He will give you the sustenance you need to maintain the course and weather the storms. The prophet Isaiah said it best when he said, "When you pass through the waters, I will be with you; and when you pass through the rivers, they will not sweep over you. When you walk through the fire, you will not be burned; the flames will not set you ablaze." (Is. 43:2)

## Don't Bury Your Talent

God has given each one of us talents. To some, He's given more than others, but in the end, God will not hold you accountable for the talents that you didn't have; he's only going to hold you accountable for the ones that He gave you. That ought to bring about a check in your spirit asking, "Have I been faithful with what I've been entrusted with?"

Many people will never reach their fullest potential, go to the grave with unsung songs, or see God's plans unfold because the cost of getting there is too high. Anything of great value will come with a significant cost, which most people want to avoid paying. They're ready to pay for the CliffsNotes and the Genie Passes to get them to the front of the line, but they're unwilling to endure for the long haul.

> **Anything of great value will come with a significant cost, which most people want to avoid paying.**

Before planting this church, I told my wife I was done with ministry. I wasn't done with Jesus or His bride, but I was done working for His bride, the church. After sixteen or so years in pastoral ministry, ranging from youth pastor to campus pastor to lead pastor, I was done with it. In the process of ministry, I contracted a disease called "sick-a-dis," and basically what that means is that "I was sick of this" ministry thing. I was exhausted from working for toxic leaders and toxic churches. My last ministry position had crushed me in what I felt was beyond repair. I thought the system was flawed and would always stay the same.

After I resigned from my last church, I started looking for jobs, which was going on in the middle of the pandemic. I would surely be a great candidate for a high-level management position. Well, I was wrong. For months, I couldn't get anyone to call me back. I got so desperate that I even applied to be the door greeter at the gym I now go to, and they didn't call me back. If there was one thing I knew I was good at, it was hospitality.

Things went like this for months and months, and I knew why. I had thrown in the towel on my call and dream, and God was throwing it back. He closed all the doors I ran to to get me back in alignment with His will for my life. It's like He put the spiritual bumpers on the bowling lane to ensure that I didn't go too far to the right or too far to the left but that I was reminded of the trajectory of His will for my life. In hindsight, I'm grateful that He did. I'm also thankful that I didn't throw away the call or the dream I had. If I had quit, I would have missed out on today's beauty: getting to pastor the church we planted called The Collective. I was tired of the journey and the process, and I started to feel like it was too much, but little did I know that the land flowing with milk and honey was just on the other side of this trial.

## Don't Give Up

In the book of James, James speaks about our trials, not just any trials; he's talking about the "sudden trials." What are the "sudden trials?" These are the trials that come upon us suddenly that we didn't do anything to bring upon us (James 1:2-4). He tells us to consider it pure joy when faced with them. Why does he say that? Well, he says that these trials have come to test your faith.

They've come to see what you're made of. They come to expose your faith and trust in God; to determine whether you possess the faith to be trusted.

James continues by saying that testing your faith will produce in you perseverance that nothing else can. This means that God needs to know that you won't get going when things get tough. He wants to ensure that you will still trust and keep going when the heat turns up. It's the art of endurance that produces Godly maturity in you. That's really what it's all about.

God is more concerned with who you become along the journey than with the destination. He desires that you be mature and complete and not lack anything because where you're going will require much of you, and to whom much is given, much is required. This is why He gives you the vision first and then leads you through the valley of humility. It's the training ground for character-building, fruit-bearing, maturing, and for building that muscle that I like to call "endurance."

No matter what may come your way—hell or high water—stay faithful to your lane, stay loyal to your talents, and live this life with unspeakable joy because maybe, just maybe, your breakthrough is on the other side of this season.

In Galatians 6:9, Paul reminds us of the reward if we don't give up. He says, "Let us not become weary in doing good, for at the proper time we will reap a harvest if we do not give up."

Did you hear that? He is giving us a written conditional promise, inspired by The Holy Spirit, that you can take to the bank. If you don't give up, you'll reap that harvest in your life you've been on the journey toward. If you don't give up on your kids, if you don't give up on your marriage, if you don't give up on your dream, if you don't give up on God, your reward will come in the form of a harvest. Don't give up! Harvest time could be around the corner.

## Reflection Questions

1. Have you ever failed as a leader? If so, how did that make you feel, and how did you respond to that season?
2. What talents or talents do you have, and are you using them appropriately?
3. Have you wanted to give up on the assignment? If so, how can you encourage yourself today to keep going and trust God for the harvest?

# FAILURE IS NECESSARY FOR SUCCESS

*I have not failed. I've just found 10,000 ways that won't work.*
–Thomas A. Edison

*Success is stumbling from failure to failure with no loss of enthusiasm.*
–Winston S. Churchill

*I've missed more than 9,000 shots in my career. I've lost almost three hundred games. Twenty-six times, I've been trusted to take the game-winning shot and missed. I've failed over and over and over again in my life. And that is why I succeed.*
–Michael Jordan

I can relate to Michael Jordan in this quote. I've never played for the Bulls or in the NBA, for that matter, but I, too, have had my fair share of failures. So, in the great words of Usher, "This is my confession."

I failed. Yup! I failed. Not just once, not just twice, but several times before, and the reality is that I'll fail again. When people say that failure is not an option, I don't know if they know what they're saying. Before rockets get launched into space, several test launches are performed to mitigate failures, and it's through those failures that they learn what needs to be fixed and adjusted before placing humans on it.

Before a new model car is sold in the showroom, several safety tests and inspections are done to determine what works and fails. They do this to make the necessary adjustments to offer the best and safest possible product.

I wonder if anyone ever talks about how to deal with failure. Most of the time, leaders talk about it being a necessary part of the process...failure. Yet, I don't ever hear about how they dealt with failure. What did they do to pick themselves back up? What did they do when they realized that they failed? How did it affect them? So many questions and so few answers.

Failure is not easy, but it is often a necessary part of your process. It is also tricky when it's out in front of the world for everyone to see and take notes. With social media, everyone can access people's business at all times. Failure is difficult to swallow when you realize that what you set out to do did not pan out how you envisioned it.

I've had several failures before coming to know Jesus and, more recently, in my faith walk with Jesus. As someone in pastoral ministry for over sixteen years, I've been dealt my hand with failures. Here's the thing about failure: it's not easy to admit. In your mind, you try to create alternative scenarios as to why what you were leading or building did not fail. You walk in denial and look to find a truth that makes you more conformable and allows you to sleep better at night. You look to blame others because surely you're not the reason. When you finally take a deep look in the mirror and come to the hard conclusion that maybe it was you, it is the moment that you can start growing into the next season of your life and journey.

Now let's get back to what I stated at the beginning of this chapter: I failed. I planted a church in the heart of Hollywood, and I failed. How exactly did I fail? Well, I failed to enjoy the process. Not enjoying the process, I developed a pessimistic mindset and unhealthy grind. I took responsibility for God and attempted to strip it from His hands so that I could control all of the elements because God was not moving at the pace that I needed Him to. He wasn't making things happen the way I pictured them in my mind.

## A Hard Reality

I failed because I was too young and inexperienced to lead a church. I wasn't fully ready to lead people to the capacity they needed to be led because I was still trying to figure out how to lead myself and my family. I didn't possess the character or the maturity to sustain the weight of what being a church planter and a pastor came with.

I failed because I thought I competed. With who? Well, myself. I felt like I had something to prove. The only way I could prove it was to succeed in such a way that I proved others wrong. Who were the others? I have no idea. I think I made up scenarios and played them out like a bad movie on repeat.

I struggled with my past and my process of becoming a pastor. I didn't take the ordinary route as many do when they feel called to pastoral ministry. I didn't grow up in the church or attend the four-year Christian University. I ran as far away from God because I knew He was calling me to something more profound than what I wanted to commit to. I wanted to be in the fashion industry, so I went to school in New York and Los Angeles to study fashion.

While getting into the industry and being around the people, I got myself caught up in a party lifestyle that led to addiction issues. Issues that almost took me out permanently. I guess being an ex-drug addict and taking the path that I took at twenty-two years of age made me feel incredibly insecure. I was trying to compensate for my lack of security in myself and God.

It was because of my deep-rooted insecurities and need to compensate for my shortcomings that I needed to fail. I needed to have my ego crushed. I needed to be broken to be built back up whole and complete, not lacking anything. I needed to understand that God does use this world's foolish things to confound the wise. Let me tell all of you something…I was a fool for sure before Jesus.

The reason that I failed in my first church planting journey was that the church that we launched is no longer in existence today. The church didn't make it after we transitioned out as the lead pastors, which was heartbreaking.

Now, did God still use that season? Of course, He did. Did God still allow us to reach people for the sake of the Gospel? Of course, He did. Did we see some incredible things take place? Of course, we did. Did we make some wonderful lifelong friends? We sure did.

Why? Because despite my shortcomings and my insecurities, He would still use all of this to shape me and mold me into the person He was leading me to become. He was still working all things together for my good. He has a way of using these moments for His glory. He also loves His people way more than I could.

What about you? Have you failed at anything yet? Have you failed and not gotten back up? Have you failed and tried again? In Aliyah's words, "If at first you don't succeed, you can dust yourself off and try again..try again."

Most people never fail because they never dare to step out in faith and try in the first place, which, in all honesty, is a failure anyway. Many of us live in the "what if this doesn't work" realm, where we spend so much time imagining the worst possible scenarios if we step out in faith to accomplish our God-given dreams and potential.

Many people will go to the grave with unsung songs (I mentioned this in a previous chapter, but it was too good not to repeat). Many of us will pass this life with a dream still in our hearts. Why? Because we were too afraid of the "what if I fail?"

Here's a hard truth: You might fail—you'll probably fail several times—but you'll learn so much. You'll know what it means to be resilient. You'll learn what it means to depend on God more than ever; it means understanding the art of longevity and faithfulness.

Failure is key! It's the key to success. If you have yet to fail, then you haven't tried to do anything complicated, so look at the story of Steve Jobs. He started in a garage with just one other person, and now Apple is a two billion dollar company with over 4,000

MOST PEOPLE
NEVER FAIL
BECAUSE THEY
NEVER DARE TO
STEP OUT IN
FAITH AND TRY
IN THE FIRST
PLACE, WHICH
IN ALL HONESTY,
IS A FAILURE
ANYWAY.

FAILURE IS NECESSARY FOR SUCCESS

employees. We all know that Steve Jobs did not take Apple to where it is overnight. He was fired from the very company that he began. It was his dismissal that led him to realize that his passion for his work exceeded the disappointment and failure he encountered. Eventually, Steve went to work for two other companies and had great success, which brought him back to the CEO position at Apple. Steve Jobs said, "I didn't see it then, but it turned out that getting fired from Apple was the best thing that could have ever happened to me." Failure was the very thing during the process that eventually led him to his success.

I think that sometimes God allows failure to see how we're going to respond to it, to determine whether we are hungry for that thing, we're going after, to see if we're willing to give it our all until the very end, to see if our heart is really in the right place. Let me tell you something about failure: It exposes many things in our hearts, and motives are one of them. Failure is the necessary ingredient to the recipe for success.

> **Failure is the necessary ingredient to the recipe for success.**

### Willing To Fail

What would you do right now if you were fearless in failing? What's that dream in your heart sitting in park, waiting for the right conditions before you launch into the deep? News flash! If you're waiting for the right conditions, you will be waiting a long time.

The Israelites were told to cross the Jordan at flood stage when it was at its highest to step into their promised land. Spoiler alert...

they made it across because it stopped flowing once the feet of the priest hit the water. God tested them to see if they would trust, obey, and take the first step.

God is waiting for some of you to take the first step. I know what you're thinking. You're thinking, "Alberto, you have no idea what's in my heart and how scary it is." That is true, I don't, but what I do know is that I'd rather put my feet into the Jordan to see if God was going to move instead of sitting on the banks of the Jordan staring at what could have been while wondering and living in the "what if?"

Here's the crazy part: the Israelites made several attempts to get to the Promised Land, but they failed many times before for several reasons. Their failures led to their success. The people who didn't make it were people who struggled to trust and believe. The people who made it were those who had learned from the failures of those before them.

Your failure today might not bring success for you, but it might bring success for the next generation. As a father, I know my children will learn several lessons independently because of their failures and mistakes. If I can minimize the number of those failures because they know from mine and save them time, then it's a win for me in the end.

How did I handle the realization that I failed? Not well! It honestly sucked. It wasn't enjoyable. It was a feeling I didn't like at the moment, and I never wanted to feel that way again. I think that I took that failure and wanted to hide. I tried to hide from my peers, friends, and close circle. I wanted to disappear off the face of the planet, but I didn't.

I had to accept it and come to terms with it. I had a lot of processing to do, but eventually, I saw it through a different lens. It gave me the fuel that I needed to keep going and make changes along the way. It gave me more tools to add to my belt and tools I knew how to use now. It developed something undeniable in me: a fierce passion for loving harder, leading better, and trusting more.

What did I learn from that season now that I'm leading a new church as the lead pastor? I learned to value the journey more than the destination. I learned that God calls me to be obedient and allow Him to bring about the fruit. I learned that part of the process is learning to have joy while in it. Joy is the art of finding a reason for gladness despite your circumstances. I learned that people are not objects to be used as a means to an end. I learned that my failure didn't define me but refined who I was created to be. I learned that I have nothing to prove to myself, nothing to prove to others, and nothing to prove to God because I'm already approved as His child.

## Advice When Encountering Failure

1.  Ask God what He is trying to do in you. Ten times out of ten, there is a lesson that He's trying to convey to you, and He could be using this failure as a teaching moment.
2.  Evaluate your process to determine whether something needs to change. This is always a great time to take inventory and consider whether your approach needs to change.
3.  Check your attitude and healthily process your emotions. Talk to someone, process with a mentor, a therapist, or a friend. Whatever you do, don't keep it inside and allow bitterness and resentment to fester and build its home in your heart.

4.  Don't stay down. Failure is not a sign that it's over for you; it's just a detour that will get you on the right track to your destination.

5.  Don't worry about the onlookers and the commentator section of life. If you live your life worried about what others will think and say, then you should give up right now.

Don't allow the fear of failure or a past failure to hinder you from stepping up and stepping out again. Andy Stanley said, "Where there is fear, there is opportunity. Where there is greater fear, there is greater opportunity." Let that marinate for a minute. The greater the level of fear, the greater the level of opportunity! Step out today in faith! God has your back!

## Reflection Questions:

1.  Have you ever failed at anything that marked you? If so, what was it, and how do you plan to overcome that fear?

2.  What's the fear that could be holding you back today? How can you push past that fear and step into God's plan for your life?

3.  What would you do and why if fear of failure was not an option?

# 5

# THE PRODIGAL LEADER

*People change when they hurt enough that they have to change,
learn enough that they want to change, receive enough that
they are able to change.*
–John C. Maxwell

When I was a child, I loved playing the game Monopoly with my family. I secretly wanted to be a real estate mogul; maybe that's why I went to real estate school, but that's another story for another day.

Monopoly is a game of skill with a bit of chance thrown into it. There was a whole deck of cards called "chance cards." The goal was to go around the board and purchase property, build housing and hotels, collect money, and try not to go to jail.

My favorite "chance card" to get whenever I landed on the "chance" square piece was the one that would allow me to skip all of the remaining steps and go straight to "GO" to complete my $200. I loved this piece so much because it cut out the process of rolling the dice repeatedly while moving my piece and waiting my turn. This took me all the way around the board and straight to the money. I was able to cut the time and the process.

This reminds me of the story of the Prodigal Son, who tried to do the same thing. He tried to cut the line, cut the process, and go straight to collect his hyperbole $200. The only difference between him and me was that he needed the process to deepen his character so that he could handle his inheritance.

## Let Me Skip the Process Please

Give me my portion of the inheritance and give it to me now! Sound familiar? Well, it's the conversation between the Prodigal Son and his Father. Who talks to their dad that way anyway? Many of us, at some point, have found ourselves in this position, perhaps even in our relationship with our Heavenly Father.

You might be thinking to yourself right now that you have never spoken to God that way, but let's reflect. Remember when Jesus taught us how to pray and said that we should pray, "Your will be done on earth as it is in heaven"? Yeah, my prayers, if I could just be honest, were usually God, please do this and please do that, and God open this door, and then when you're done, open up this other one over here.

Okay, that is an exaggeration, but you now get the point. So often, when we pray, we seldom factor in God's will for our lives and usually pray for our will to be blessed by Him.

Consider how often we find ourselves in the shoes of the Prodigal Son. I'm not referring to a literal departure from Christ but rather a deviation from His perfect will. It's a reminder that God has a permissible will and a perfect will, and our choices can lead us astray from His best for us. But the beauty is that even in our deviations, there is always room for growth and learning.

Let's delve deeper into the concept of God's will. His permissible will refers to what He allows in our lives, even if it's not part of His perfect will. His perfect will, on the other hand, is the ideal outcome that results from our complete surrender to Him and our obedience to the Holy Spirit's guidance on our journey.

I want to examine the story of the prodigal son from a different perspective. It's not a new perspective; it's just a different one.

Imagine the Prodigal Son, living in the safety and comfort of his Father's estate. He had his responsibilities, but he was under the loving care of his Father. Unbeknownst to him, he was working a land that would one day be his. How he handled his tasks during that season would determine what he would receive when he handed them over to his Father.

Be careful because what you despise right now could be what God will give you in the future. How you take care of it now will produce fruit for you.

> **Be careful because what you despise right now could be what God will give you in the future.**

The Prodigal Son found himself in the Father's perfect will, yet he was discontent. This discontentment didn't suddenly appear one morning. It was a gradual process, a result of a distorted perspective that was challenged somewhere along his journey. This misalignment with God's will led to his discontentment, and ultimately, his loss.

Satan is crafty. He's like a serpent in the middle of the garden, trying to challenge your view of God and what He's given you, getting you to feel that there's more that God is holding out on and that you can access instantly. Someone reading this is in the right place at the right time, but your perspective has been challenged, and you've grown discontent.

Remember, your discontentment isn't a sign that God wants to transition you but rather a symptom of misalignment. It's crucial to realign yourself with God's perfect will, and I hope that by the end of this chapter, you'll be on that path.

Okay, now back to the Prodigal Son. He was right where he

needed to be, but he wanted more. I think that his desire for more was a Godly thing. We are all created to long for greater and for more. It's what keeps us motivated, and it's something that God has constructed within the core of our spiritual DNA. I mean, He has set eternity in the hearts of man. No one can fathom what God has done from beginning to end (Ecc. 3:11). All that means is that we are all knit with this desire to question the existence of our creator and that we can't even wrap our minds around what God has done and what He's going to do.

The thing with the desire to do more is that if we lack the maturity to steward it or navigate it with wisdom, it has the potential to lead us in the wrong direction or the right direction at the wrong time. Nothing is worse than having the right gifts but being in the wrong season.

But his desire for more led him astray when he decided to act on it. He boldly approached his Father, demanding his share of the inheritance immediately. In truth, the Prodigal Son was settling. How so? An inheritance grows over time, like a seed that blossoms into a tree. He wanted his share of the estate before it had fully matured... and before he had fully matured.

He was settling for a partial blessing instead of the full blessing. Why? His perspective got the best of him, and he thought he knew better and that now was his time to shine. This is already a recipe for disaster.

## A Recipe for Disaster

Let me share a personal anecdote to illustrate this point. When my wife and I first got married, she had no idea how to cook. Our first week as a married couple was a week of recipe experiments. This

NOTHING IS WORSE THAN HAVING THE RIGHT GIFTS BUT BEING IN THE WRONG SEASON.

**THE PRODIGAL LEADER**

experience taught us the importance of patience and learning from our mistakes, just like the Prodigal Son had to learn the hard way.

One day, when I arrived from work, she greeted me in the doorway of our apartment with the biggest Kool-Aid smile I had ever seen. I asked her what she was so happy about, and she told me that she had made dinner and that it was ready. Honestly, I was super excited and rushed to the dinner table.

As I sat down, she served my plate, stacked white rice with another massive scoop of what we Cubans call "picadillo." The smell was that of my grandmother's house when I was growing up. It smelled like Little Havana in my home.

I remember she dropped the plate before me and wanted to watch me take the first bite, so I did. I jammed a giant scoop of food my fork would hold into my mouth. At that moment, I realized we had a problem… a considerable problem. The bite I put into my mouth was about the saltiest thing I had ever tasted. I drank enough water at that moment to send the entire state of California into a drought.

Upon investigating the reason for the food's saltiness, I found out that Ashley didn't know that garlic salt had salt in it, so she added salt to the food. The recipe called for garlic powder, but she used garlic salt instead. The food had double the salt that the recipe called for, which meant it was a recipe for disaster.

In the same way, the Prodigal Son had already begun what was aiming to be a recipe for disaster. He wanted what was rightfully his but at the wrong time. See, the inheritance would come later in his life, most likely at the passing of his Father. This means that the Prodigal Son would have been older, more experienced, more mature, and more able to handle the immensity of the inheritance.

As stated above, the inheritance would have also matured and grown in interest.

It was a recipe for disaster because he didn't have the tools to manage or sustain the immensity of the inheritance he requested; hence, he spent it on wild living. We know that in the end, he returned home, and Father welcomed him with open arms and established him back in his position. He ended up right back where he started.

I can only imagine the aspect of humility that it took and taught him to come back and be back. Call me crazy, but the Prodigal Son wanted his promise without going through the process. He tried to skip steps to get what he thought he wanted. He tried to play Monopoly with his life and chance his blessing. You can only get to a promise with a process. A process will always precede a promise.

> **You can only get to a promise with a process. A process will always precede a promise.**

## Are You Ready For More?

Maybe you have settled for something less than the fullness of what God desires to give you out of impatience.

I can't tell you how much I can relate to this story. I can't even begin to tell you how many times I thought I was ready for the more; I felt I was prepared for the platform or was ready to lead on my own. That Prodigal Son mindset set me on a journey of God's permissible will versus God's perfect will.

I was a youth pastor and thought I was ready to lead at a higher level I was not prepared for. I knew I was created for more and wanted to do more, but it wasn't my time. I wanted my inheritance, and I liked it now. My decision to leave and step into a new season would lead me on the ride of my life, and I can honestly say that God gave me everything I asked for, and it almost ruined me.

It almost ruined me because I didn't have the maturity, character, or wisdom to sustain the weight of what I had asked for. I truly believe that God brought me to the very thing that I thought I wanted for me to realize that I didn't like that. I realized that much of what I wanted was out of selfish ambition and not Kingdom. It was gifting without the infrastructure to sustain it.

Maybe you're there right now. You're in a season where you're living with a tension between two realities. The reality is your current assignment and the desire for the truth you envision manifesting now. If we can learn anything from The Prodigal Son or my experience, it would be to learn to pray that His will be done and not yours. It would be for you to understand the art of contentment in the season that you are in because it's in that season that you will develop the character to substation the fullness of God's promise for your life.

When Paul said that he had learned the art of contentment in every situation, whether he was well-fed or hungry. Whether he had plenty or he lacked, he had learned how to be content through it all. The question is, what was that contentment? How did Paul know it? Well, it was probably through experience, but the word contentment just meant that it was the sufficiency of Christ. What does that mean? It means that it was always about Christ, it never stopped being about Him, and it would never stop being about Him.

Sometimes, our season is all about emptying us of ourselves so that He can fully inhabit our lives to the desired degree.

Paul said that no matter what I'm going through in life, I can be content because it's all about Jesus, and my focus will not be on me or my circumstances but on the Author and the Finisher of my faith, Jesus. Sometimes, our season is all about emptying us of ourselves so that He can fully inhabit our lives to the desired degree.

Jesus said that He doesn't cast pearls before swine. You might be asking, did he call me a pig? The answer is maybe... just kidding. Jesus essentially says that He doesn't give things of high value to those who can't value or steward them.

You may be wondering why your time hasn't come yet, and my response is that it hasn't come because it's not that time yet. It is time for you to adopt the proper perspective to see the beauty of what God has you in the middle of. He has called you to do what only you can do right now.

You are under the covering of the Father, and that's the best place to be. If you've veered away, maybe it's time to return home, wherever that is. It could just be that home is waiting for you to return because you're not done yet, and home has something you need before stepping into the fullness of your inheritance.

## Reflection Questions:

1. Do you feel that your process has been slow as you've stepped out toward your dream? If so, how have you managed it?
2. How can you begin to be content in your season and in your process?
3. What steps have you tried to skip along the process and how do you see God trying to bring you back around to them?

# 6

# WHO LIED TO YOU?

*You are the only you God made... God made you and
broke the mold.*
–Max Lucado

*Remember always that you not only have the right to be an
individual, you have an obligation to be one.*
–Eleanor Roosevelt

'm originally from Los Angeles and live in Bakersfield, California. Bakersfield and Los Angeles could not be any more different. Los Angeles is a big city that's always on the move with the hustle and bustle of life. It's the concrete jungle filled with all the things that city life comes with. On the other hand, Bakersfield is a smaller, slower-paced city from which much of our agriculture comes. Central California is the motherland of agriculture, and that's where I am.

I'm not much of a farmer-type guy, although I told my mother I wanted to be a farmer when I was four. During the pandemic, I tried to put my nonexistent farming skills to use, so I planted a garden. I started with zucchini and strawberries, but for the story's sake, let's focus on the zucchini. I've never planted anything except for that lima bean in the third grade, but I was determined. I went to Home Depot, bought the seeds and some soil, and went to work. I got home, poured out the soil, turned it over and over, and then buried the zucchini seeds like a boss.

To my absolute surprise, a few weeks later, I not only had zucchini, but I had giant zucchini. I'm talking colossal-sized zucchini. I couldn't believe it. I had finally lived out my dream of becoming a farmer at four years old. I was honestly shocked that it worked. That I was able to grow something. What got me was that such a tiny seed could produce something significant with time. When buried into the ground and nurtured with the correct elements, the tiny seed produced a harvest of zucchini that I couldn't keep up with. It all started with a seed.

## Don't Believe the Lies

So many things in life start small and then blossom into something big. In the very same way, Satan's entire ploy is to plant a seed or seeds of lies into your mind in the hopes that something would stick and grow into something unhealthy that causes you harm along the line. He's been seed-planting lies into humanity from day one.

The scriptures declare that "he was a murderer from the beginning, not holding to the truth, for there is no truth in him. When he lies, he speaks his native language, for he is a liar and the father of lies" (Jn. 8:44).

His native language is lying. It's what he does best. I believe that the greatest threat to our lives and leadership is believing a lie about ourselves, our situation, or others that causes us great distress, depression, anxiety, fear, and the list can go on and on.

He lied to the angels in heaven, and a third of them were cast out to hell by God. He lied to Adam and Eve and caused them to doubt God's truth, which led to the fall of humanity, and he lies to you daily. It all begins as a tiny seed, though. If we allow that seed to take root in our minds and grow, it can be the spiritual death of us.

The Bible says, "For as he thinketh in his heart, so he is" (Proverbs 23:7 KJV). You become what you believe about yourself. Satan, knowing this, uses it to his advantage to trip you up. The thing to take notice of is that the scripture points to the heart instead of to the mind. It could have read, "For as he thinketh in his mind, so he is," but that's not what it says. What does it mean to "think in your heart?'

We have to look at it from the beginning. We have to determine where the origin of the thought came from. The idea first comes to our minds. When the seed is planted, we have two options. We can either marinate on that thought, replay it repeatedly, or evict it and tell it that it has to go. When we choose not to evict the thought and dwell on it, eventually, that thought makes its way to our hearts. In your heart is where you get your emotions from. It's the place that brings all of the feelings. It's also the thing that can be wicked and deceitful, according to Jeremiah.

> **When the seed is planted, we have two options. We can either marinate on that thought, replay it repeatedly, or evict itand tell it that it has to go.**

## Check Your Emotions at the Door

Once the thought goes from your mind to your heart, it becomes an emotion. That emotion can be anything, such as anger, fear, rage, or anxiety, and it can also lead to joy, happiness, peace, etc. Once that thought turns into an emotion, that emotion manifests in our actions. This means that the emotion comes out, and we live through the lens of that emotion. Once that happens, we create our world through what we live out. Proverbs 4:23 says, "Guard your heart above all else, for it determines the course of your life." This is why guarding our thoughts and thought life is so important.

> **Once that thought turns into an emotion that emotion manifests in our actions.**

Some of you reading this book have quite possibly been living a lie your entire life, and you don't even know it. I don't mean that you're living in secret sin. What I mean is that somewhere along your life journey, someone said something to you or did something to you, and that moment, whether you realize it or not, marked you and could have been traumatic. From that day, you could have attached yourself to a lie from that incident.

For example, maybe a parent told you that you weren't good enough as a child, and because of that, you live with very low self-esteem and are critical of others who do great things. Maybe that thought has marked you and caused you to miss out on some incredible moments in life.

Maybe you're a cynical person. You always have a negative view of things before they even start. You may be wondering where did that come from? At some point in your life, you faced great disappointment from someone close to you, which marked you. That moment killed any level of high expectations you carried, and so, in response to that, you've lost hope in humanity and believe the absolute worst about anything and everything. Why? Maybe you thought a lie that everyone in life would disappoint you, but you should live a life that's already disappointing so you won't ever get hurt again.

It's the lies we believe that hold us back from freedom, create our world, and keep us from stepping into everything God has for us. This is why it's so important to know how the devil works, understand what you're up against, and combat the lies when they do come your way.

IT'S THE LIES WE BELIEVE THAT HOLD US BACK FROM **FREEDOM**, CREATE OUR WORLD, AND KEEP US FROM STEPPING INTO EVERY-THING GOD HAS FOR US.

WHO LIED TO YOU?

Growing up in a Hispanic household is terrific. I loved it, and I love my culture, but one thing about Cubans is that they'll take your most tremendous insecurity and turn it into your nickname. As a kid, I was chubby, so my family called me "Gordo" as a nickname. That means "fatty." It's not that they were being malicious or evil; it was their way of showing love.

That name followed me throughout my adulthood, even when I was skinny. At that point, the damage was already done. I always thought I was overweight, no matter how fit I was. Why? I chose to believe a lie I had heard my whole life, which informed my thinking and emotions. I lived thinking that I was always overweight. Now, I don't believe that anymore, but the things that we latch onto, if we're not careful, can cause us some harm.

## What Lie Have You Believed?

Have you believed a lie about yourself? Have you been living a life informed by misinformed emotions? Many leaders are living in fear, insecurity, and anxiety because of the lies that they've believed about themselves and even their ministries.

For instance, you might feel like you're not good enough to lead, not relevant enough to make a difference, not cool enough to connect with your peers, or not smart enough to understand complex theological concepts. All of these are common self-limiting beliefs, but sadly, many have fallen prey to them.

Like many, I've also grappled with these thoughts that try to invade my mind. But here's the thing, I don't let them take root. I actively work to dispel them and keep them from lingering. Yes, there are days when the lies seem to shout louder, but once you recognize them for what they are, it empowers you to redefine how you see yourself and your leadership.

Today could be the day you break free from this cycle. Perhaps today is the day you remove that seed of doubt and cast it away, allowing you to walk in the truth and freedom that Christ has for you. The potential for personal growth and transformation is within your reach.

God gives us the practical tools to overcome the lies of the devil supernaturally. There are four sensible approaches to getting your mind right and aligning with what God says about you:

1.  ***You have to recognize that in Jesus, you have the mind of Christ.***

    I Corinthians 2:16 tells us that we have the mind of Christ. What does that even mean? It means you can know the difference between the two voices fighting for real estate in your mind. You can know when God is speaking truth to you and when the devil is casting lies at you.

    To have the mind of Christ means that you're now able to see things from His perspective. You get to view your life, situations, trials, good moments, and bad moments through the lens of truth. This means that you can see things the way that God sees them. You can respond to things the way you should, living a life that bears the fruit of the spirit.

2.  ***You have to read the playbook.***

    What's the playbook? The Bible. The only way you'll be able to identify a lie is by first knowing the truth. Here's the truth: most Christians don't know what the Bible says outside of what the preacher preaches on Sunday. Most believers don't see what God says about them and how God views them. Most believers don't even know God's promise for them through a life of obedience. If you don't see the truth, you'll believe a lie quicker than you think. You dispel a lie when you align it with the truth.

> ## You dispel a lie when you align it with the truth.

I worked in retail and constantly dealt with money at the register. Sometimes, people would try to use counterfeit bills. They would do it by slipping a fake bill in the middle of the actual bills. I'm not trying to brag on myself, but I was spot on when detecting a counterfeit bill. Why? Because I handled real money all day, I knew what it felt like, smelled, and looked like. This means I could quickly identify any fake bill when someone tried to throw it in the middle of actual bills. It might have looked natural and smelled real, but in the end, it never felt real.

Spotting fraud can be easy when you are used to dealing with it on a regular basis. Similarly, reading and immersing yourself in the Word of God can help you recognize His truth and love more easily. This means that whenever the devil tries to deceive you with a lie, you will be able to spot it and reject it. In Romans 12:2 (NLT), we are reminded to not conform to the ways of the world, but to let God transform us by renewing our minds. By doing so, we can learn God's will for our lives, which is good, pleasing, and perfect.

We can change our thought patterns by filling our minds with new thoughts from the Word of God. The Bible can reprogram our

THE BIBLE CAN REPROGRAM OUR THOUGHT LIFE

TO BE FILLED WITH FAITH, HOPE, AND LOVE.

WHO LIED TO YOU?

thought life to be filled with faith, hope, and love. Falling in love with the Word of God can truly change our lives. In Joshua 1:8, the Lord tells Joshua to continually study the Book of Instruction, meditate on it day and night, and obey everything written in it. Only then will he prosper and succeed in all he does.

Joshua prepared for war and led God's people into the Promised Land. To ensure success and prosperity, he had to meditate on God's Word and live it out. "Meditate on it" in the original language means to "read in an undertone, speak, and proclaim." With that being said, what was God trying to tell Joshua? He was saying, "Joshua, read my Word to yourself, speak my Word over yourself, your family, and the people you are leading, and then proclaim my Word over all of it. There is power in reading, speaking, and proclaiming the Word over your life. The tongue has the power of life and death, so it is better to speak truth and life over yourself and your situations than anything else."

**There is power in reading the Word, speaking the Word, and proclaiming the Word over your life.**

3. *Identify the lie through self-awareness and serve it an eviction notice.*

   To identify a lie, you need to be self-aware. However, you can only achieve self-awareness if you have completed the necessary steps beforehand. Once you know the truth, you will be more aware of the devil and his tricks. After recognizing the lie, you need to tell yourself that you won't believe it this time.

Then, you must serve it an eviction notice and tell it to leave. II Corinthians 10:5 says, "We demolish arguments and every pretension that sets itself up against the knowledge of God, and we take captive every thought to make it obedient to Christ."

That means you take any negative thought that doesn't align with God's Word and will for your life, bring it to Christ, and align it with His Word. If it doesn't align with the truth, send it packing and on its way out.

## 4. *Walk in freedom*

Christ has set you free. Free in all areas of your life, not just a few. That means you have the freedom to control what you allow to stick. Christ can dispel all the lies that you've believed in your life that have hindered you, as well as all the future lies that the devil will attempt to plant along the way.

It may be time to start telling yourself that you can do this. You can start that business, attend that church, start that podcast, have a healthy marriage, and have children who love the Lord. You are more than a conqueror in Jesus!

Do you believe it? I do for you!

**Reflection Questions:**

1. Reflect on a time when you faced a challenge or a difficult situation and were able to overcome it. How did you handle it, and what was the outcome?
2. Think about a situation where you encountered negativity or false beliefs from others. How did you respond to it, and what did you learn from the experience?
3. Consider a time when you felt doubt or fear due to negative thoughts or external influences. How did you manage these emotions, and what strategies did you use to overcome them?
4. Reflect on your own thought patterns and emotional responses. Are there any recurring negative thoughts or emotions that you tend to dwell on? How do they impact your actions and decisions?
5. In what ways do you guard your heart and mind from negative influences? What practices or habits do you employ to ensure that you maintain a healthy thought life?

# 7

# SUBMIT OR SPLIT

*Change is the law of life and those who look only to the past or present are certain to miss the future.*
–John F. Kennedy

*Change will not come if we wait for some other person or some other time. We are the ones we've been waiting for. We are the change that we seek.*
–Barack Obama

Have you ever hosted a party or gathering at your house only to have that one guest who didn't leave after everyone else? There's always one who tends to overstay their welcome, and they need help to read the room or get the social cues you're putting in. You say things such as, "Look at the time; I have work early tomorrow morning," or you ask them a question such as, "Aren't you tired?" Yet, they still don't get the clue. I'm sure that this has happened to all of us, and some of you reading right now are that person. We still love you, though.

It's crucial to recognize the signs of overstaying one's welcome in a job, church, or relationship. I've often encountered pastors and leaders who, despite their misery in their current roles, cling on, subjecting themselves and their families to unnecessary hardship in the hope of a change that may never come.

I have a saying I picked up early on in ministry: You have two options when working anywhere. You can either submit or split, but you can't be in the middle of either one.

## Overstayed My Welcome

During the early years of my ministry, I worked as a youth pastor at my first church, located in the inner city of Los Angeles. I cherished everything about that place, from my beloved students to the city itself. I had established strong connections with business owners and city officials, and our youth group hosted the very first annual skate competition at the local skate park, which attracted 500 skater kids from all over the surrounding inner cities. I had also developed relationships with the local gang leaders and frequently ministered to them and their families. As a result, we became the largest inner city youth group in the area.

Although it was an incredible place for ministry, something was stirring in me that it was time to go. How did I know it was time to go? Well, the things that I once loved about the church I no longer cared for. I started becoming critical in my heart about decisions and moves that were being made. Mind you, there wasn't anything wrong; it was just that God was attempting to make the nest uncomfortable for me so that I would fly to the next assignment.

After a while, I no longer enjoyed what I was doing and felt weighted down by it all. Nothing had changed; a stirring came over me that I didn't quite recognize initially. No one had ever talked to me about transition and all that came with it, such as the symptoms. My wife and I were getting to a place where we thought it might be time to go. We prayed and waited. God spoke through a sequence of events and talked to me through my wife. We reached a point where we could no longer serve the vision of the house. We didn't disrespect our pastor or team but knew we couldn't stay.

One day, I tried to resign, as my wife and I had discussed, but when I went to do it, I choked and couldn't go through with it. I was convinced that I needed to stay longer. Let me just tell you that staying longer turned out to be a massive season of strain on me and on our marriage. I felt like the heat got turned up, and I was getting crushed in every direction.

Why did I feel that way? Because I overstayed my welcome. I didn't take the hyperbole "social cues" from God and kept trying to make it happen. You may be wondering why did I stay so long. It's because I feared the unknown and what wasn't familiar. I didn't know if God would open a door elsewhere, and I had a new family to consider. I didn't want to take a leap of faith like God was calling me to until He opened up another door. I distinctly remember sensing in my spirit that God would not open another door until I first closed the one in front of me.

Seven months later, I resigned, and God did what He said He was going to do: He opened up another door. The irony in all of this is that the new position that I had stepped into had been vacant for seven months, and they could not find the right person until me. I felt like God graced me and held that door open for me as I navigated this new world of transition. When the transition finally took place, it was smooth and professional.

## Should I Stay or Should I Go?

You may be in a current season where you're sensing it's time to go. God has made the nest uncomfortable. You no longer love what you're doing where you're doing it. Perhaps you're working in a toxic environment with a toxic leader. Yes, I just went there. Too many churches are led by too many toxic leaders. Maybe you're at a place where you can no longer submit to leadership, and it's made things difficult for you and your family. Please note that it also affects the other departments of the leadership team when you overstay your welcome as well.

I would say to you that determining whether it's time to go is simple, and yet we overcomplicate it. Submit or Split. It's one or the other. If you can no longer submit to the leader, vision, or both, it's time to go. The longer you stay, the more miserable you will become, and all those around you will be able to sense it as well. Whether you realize it or not, overstaying your welcome and not being able to submit wholeheartedly damages the organization, the church, and yourself. It creates tension and friction between you and the lead pastor or boss or you and the board, who is your accountability. But once you recognize these signs and make the decision to leave, a sense of relief and liberation will wash over you, paving the way for a new and healthier chapter in your life.

> **If you can no longer submit to the leader, vision, or both, it's time to go.**

The longer you stay, the more unhealthy you'll become, especially if you're in a toxic environment. If damage has already been done, more damage will occur, and it will take a longer time to heal from the wounds you experience and endure. Remember, your well-being should always be a priority, and sometimes, that means making the difficult decision to leave a situation that is no longer serving you.

When people want to transition, they call me, which I find hilarious. I get calls from leaders asking me for advice and telling me how I did it when I was in their shoes. Most of the initial calls will lead to no change on their behalf. They usually overstay their welcome until the damage is done and leave by force or duress. The common denominator is, "I just don't feel like I've been released." To which I respond, "I didn't know you worked in a prison." Remember, you're not alone in this journey. Many others have faced similar challenges and have successfully navigated through them. Reach out for support and guidance when you need it.

When I hear that, I have a translation function in my head that can decipher the phrase. What I'm hearing typically is, "You mean that you don't have a job offer or know about any other openings?" That's what it boils down to. We're in the business of faith, yet we struggle to walk in faith, so we'd rather stay in misery.

I don't believe that God holds you captive to misery. Now granted, often, God will put you under a bad leader to pound out the bad leader that could be buried in your heart, but there will be a time to move on from that. I think that maybe God placed King David under King Saul because maybe, just maybe, deep within David's heart was a Saul-like element that God needed to purge. The only way to do so was to place him under someone God never wanted David to be like.

I also don't understand why leaders who worked for toxic leaders end up recreating the cycle themselves when they're the boss. Instead of learning from their season of hardship, they do the complete opposite and become the very thing that they despise. Please don't be that guy or girl!

## A Lesson Form David and Saul

While serving King Saul in the palace, David got to a place where he could no longer submit to Saul. Things were getting bad the moment that David started getting praise from the people for his wartime efforts. King Saul didn't like that and started to get jealous of David. Usually, most toxic leaders struggle with deep insecurities that they have not learned to keep at bay, which causes them to treat their staff poorly. (I have a whole chapter on this)

King Saul's emotions got the best of him, and one night, he decided to throw spears at David in hopes of killing him. What did David do when this all started taking place? He first dodged the spear so as not to get hit and die, and then he fled the kingdom for his life. Was David not fully submitted to King Saul because he fled for his life? No, David was just smart enough to know that he'd be dead if he overstayed his welcome.

You might be thinking that this is an extreme story to use for your situation but I think not. David was submitted to King Saul and his madness for a season, but when he saw that the season was over, he said, "Peace out!" David didn't wait for his LinkedIn to notify him that another king was hiring before he left. The truth is that David had nowhere to go, but he left. Not only did he leave, but he left quietly. He never grabbed the spear that probably stuck to the wall and threw it back at Saul. David quickly saw the writing on the wall. This is a powerful lesson in recognizing when a season is over and having the courage to move on, even when the future is uncertain.

Was that season of David running from King Saul difficult? Absolutely, but it's what brought him back to the palace eventually, but that time, he would be coming back as the King. You can't fear the process and not having all the pieces together. Sometimes, the "release" is the lack of health you are experiencing and witnessing. Don't overstay your welcome waiting for something else to open. Your mental and spiritual health is more important. The health of your marriage and family dynamic is more important than any ministry assignment. It is your number one ministry assignment. This is a powerful reminder to prioritize your well-being above all else, as it is the foundation upon which all other aspects of your life are built.

# THE HEALTH OF YOUR MARRIAGE AND FAMILY DYNAMIC IS

SUBMIT OR SPLIT

# MORE IMPORTANT THAN ANY MINISTRY ASSIGNMENT.

I've witnessed marriages fall apart due to the lack of communication and understanding. I've watched families torn apart because of the disagreements and conflicts, and in the end, this is not the heart of God for any of His children.

If you do decide to stay in it, you have no right to complain about it or bicker about it. Because you made the decision to remain where you are now, you now have the biblical mandate to honor the leadership and vision of the house. This could mean supporting their decisions, participating in community activities, and contributing positively to the growth of the house. In the end, God gives you the choice.

If you're waiting for the loud and thunderous voice to give you permission to leave, you'll be waiting a long time. Remember, it's the season that God is using to speak to you. This means that you have the power to know your season. You have the ability to be discerning enough to know what season you're in and what season God is leading you into next.

Now, not all transitions are bad. There might be a point when it's just your time to go; when it is, make sure you do the best possible job. Most churches do a horrible job of transitioning leaders out. Usually, pastors get offended and take the transitions personally. Then they operate from that offense that never needed to be there at all. Remember, there is no college course or road map to a healthy transition, but God gives us wisdom, the guidance of the Holy Spirit, and the Bible to show us how we ought to treat one another, which will help the transition process.

The greatest thing that we can do as leaders when we're transitioning from one space to the next is to finish strong, honor the leadership, and honor the place that we're leaving from. In the end,

# SUBMIT OR SPLIT

The greatest thing that we can do as leaders when we're transitioning from one space to the next is to **finish strong, honor the leadership, and honor the place that we're leaving from.**

it was the very place that God led you to so that He could work in you and through you.

If you're a lead pastor or a boss, the best thing you can do when someone transitions from your church or organization is not take it personally. That employee was never yours to begin with. That person was on loan from God, and your job was to steward them well in their starting and finishing. Work out a strategy that you write down and agree upon so there is clarity for you and the church or organization. Honor them for the time that they were with you and for the investment that they made. In the end, people are watching how you handle this, and from your approach, people will formulate their perspective on transition. We should be the best at it!

Through all of my experiences in transition, and I've had a lot, it's taught me what I don't want to be like and what I do want to be like. In the hardest of transitions, I've learned the most about myself and the most about the kind of leader I wanted to be. I wish I could keep my team forever, but biblically, I also have a mandate to send them off to do greater work for the kingdom. I pray that the local church would be the best at sending leaders away into their new season and raising new leaders to take their place. Seeing them off to their next assignment would be a moment of celebration.

## Reflections Questions:

1. Can you provide an example from the text that illustrates the concept of recognizing when it's time to move on from a certain position?
2. How did the author come to the realization that it was time to leave their ministry role?
3. What challenges did the author face when they realized they had overstayed their welcome?
4. According to the text, what recommendations are given to determine if it's time to move on from a certain role or environment?

# 8

# THE EMOTIONAL LEADER

*Ignoring our emotions is turning our back on reality. Listening to our emotions ushers us into reality. And reality is where we meet God. . . . Emotions are the language of the soul. They are the cry that gives the heart a voice. . .*
–Peter Scazzero

## The Email That Should Have Waited

I remember getting called into my former pastor's office one afternoon, wondering what we were going to talk about. I casually walked in like I would any other time. I didn't know what we would discuss, but I looked forward to hanging out for a few minutes with him.

I remember walking the long hallway from my office toward his with not a worry on my mind. I zipped past his secretary and smiled as I proceeded to make my way into his office. I quickly noticed he wasn't seated in his seating area, where he would have counseling sessions. This was the area where we would sit if we were shooting the breeze and having casual conversations.

He was seated behind his desk, and the chair on the other side was pulled back, ready for me to take a seat. Instantly, I knew something was wrong, and my heart began to race like a horse around the track at the Kentucky Derby. As I approached the chair, I quickly started repeating scenarios that had happened during the week where I might have messed up. Nothing came to mind, so I then talked myself off the mental ledge and told myself that this was going to be a normal conversation and that I was overreacting.

I sat down quickly and greeted my pastor with my typical greeting. Right after the words rolled off my lips, I noticed his facial expression didn't reciprocate the joy that I came in with. He had a stone-cold face, stoic as all outdoors. He didn't even flinch. At that moment, I realized I had messed up, but I couldn't pinpoint what I had done.

After I took my seat, he wasted no time jumping into the rebuke of a lifetime. He asked me about an email that I had sent that morning. By morning, he meant 2:00 a.m. As soon as he asked me the question, I could feel my stomach turn, and my sweat glands informed my pores that they needed to release an intense amount of sweat.

I didn't know he would respond to my email in such a way but let me explain first what it was all about. I felt frustrated with other staff members and their performance compared to mine. I thought he didn't care about their lack of progress or that I was working on overload.

I thought it was my duty to send him an email explaining how I felt about the whole situation and demanding that he hold them accountable the same way he held me accountable.

He didn't like that email at all. He didn't like my tone and advised me not to send emails so late at night when emotions are at an all-time high or low after a full day of work and family obligations.

He kindly rebuked me and was gracious in his approach, knowing that I was still learning and growing as a pastor and leader. He knew exactly what the issue was: I allowed my emotions to trigger me into sending a heated email that didn't have to be sent right then and there.

He was right. I was fuming that evening due to a few events that had occurred that day, and I allowed my emotions to get the best of me. I made a poor call on an emotional low.

Here's the truth: you should never make a decision on an emotional high or an emotional low. Those are the worst times to act, react, post, or hit "send" on that email or text. Why is that the case?

**YOU SHOULD NEVER
MAKE A DECISION ON
AN EMOTIONAL HIGH**



**OR AN EMOTIONAL LOW**

## The Heart Can Be Tricky

Jeremiah said that the heart is wicked and deceitful and that it cannot be trusted fully. Our heart is the feeling mechanism of our life. It's the place where our emotions come from. The thoughts we choose to entertain eventually make their way to our hearts and turn into emotions. From our emotions, we tend to make decisions that aren't always the best.

Why? Because our emotions are always up and down like the stock exchange? One minute we love something and the next minute we hate it. One minute, we love doing something, and the next minute, we hate it. Just because we feel it doesn't make it accurate.

As a leader, you will always be in a place where your emotions are high or low, depending on the situation. Whether a staff member makes you upset over something ridiculous, a congregant complains about something, or a customer treats you with disrespect, those are highly charged moments that can lead our emotions to go all over the place.

> **We tend to make permanent decisions that will have a lasting effect during temporary states of emotions.**

Your emotions can make you angry, happy, sad, anxious, suspicious, and the list can continue. It's not the wisest thing to decide in those moments. We tend to make permanent decisions that will have a lasting effect during temporary states of emotions. Many people have made irreversible decisions on emotions that they wish they could take back, but by then, it was too late.

## React or Respond

As a leader, you can either react or respond to situations. There's a difference between reacting and responding to situations. Both deal with the same problems but can produce entirely different outcomes.

The Bible says that a fool shows their annoyance at once. That means that a fool reacts to the situations they face at once without ever giving it a second thought. When you choose to make decisions out of emotions quickly, you're walking in foolishness and not operating in wisdom.

Reactionary leaders are hyper-emotional and the kinds of leaders their staff are afraid of because you never know what face you'll get each day. They're leaders who are ticking time bombs. Because of situations and outcomes, they can explode or jump up for joy at any moment without notice. Being a reactionary leader is not a mark of a mature leader.

## A Hard Truth

When I was in my late twenties and early thirties, I was a very reactionary leader. I'm passionate by nature and very charismatic. I communicate with my hands, and I can be animated when telling a story. Being Cuban just amplifies the decibel in my voice to the next level. When I was a child growing up and a friend was going to come over, I first warned them that it would sound like we were all upset at each other, but that wasn't the case. I would say that's just how Cubans are.

**REACTIONARY LEADERS ARE HYPER-EMOTIONAL AND THE KINDS OF LEADERS THEIR STAFF ARE AFRAID OF BECAUSE YOU NEVER KNOW WHAT FACE YOU'LL GET EACH DAY.**

THE EMOTIONAL LEADER

While Ashley and I were at a conference, I saw an older woman talking to her for a while at a distance from where I was standing. They talked for quite a while, and occasionally, they would both glance at me and smile. I'm not a mind reader, but it was obvious that they were talking about me.

Once they finished their conversations and parted ways, Ashley walked in my direction. I was in suspense with every step she took because I was curious about what they were discussing. At the moment, it felt like she was walking in slow motion and doing it on purpose, but it was just my anxiety.

When she finally got to me, I quickly asked her what they had been discussing. I could tell that Ashley seemed nervous and didn't want to tell me. This made me want to know all the more, so I pressed her again about the conversation. She looked at me nervously and said she didn't want me to be upset with what she was about to tell me.

I swore I wouldn't get upset, but I was already upset that it was taking so long; maybe that was the problem. I asked her again what the other woman told her, and she finally spoke. The other woman told her she loved me but worried my emotions would get the best of my leadership.

I didn't know what she meant by that, so I asked for clarification. She said that her concern was that I would be someone who always reacts to things rather than responding to them. The minute Ashley said that to me, I knew exactly what she was talking about.

Hearing those words felt like I had gotten sucker punched, but I knew that it was coming. It knocked the life out of me because she was right. What she was, without saying it, is that I was an emotional leader who allowed my emotions to get the best of me one too many times.

I used my passion, heritage, and personality as an excuse to operate how I operated. I quickly realized that something had to change, and it had to start with me. I had to grow up. I had to allow my leadership to mature in a way I hadn't thought of. In order for my leadership to mature, I first needed to mature as a person.

The crazy part about all of this was that others were able to see what I was reluctant to see: that my leadership, or lack thereof, had affected others and not in a good way.

That day, I decided to become an emotionally healthy leader and not react to problems, situations, and challenges but respond to them. When you respond versus react, you take time to make an informed decision.

A leader who responds is a leader who takes a minute to make a decision, weighing the pros and the cons. They understand the wisdom in allowing their emotions to play out until they can come to the truth and make a sound, informed, and God-sought decision. The Bible says that we are to be slow to speak and slow to become angry. This truth, when embraced, enlightens us and holds so much weight across all aspects of our lives, from our marriages, relationships, with our children, our coworkers, employees, and the list can go on.

> **A leader who responds is a leader who takes a minute to make a decision.**

I've had to take a new approach to my leadership, and it's been the best thing I could have ever done. It's made a difference in me, my team, my church, and my home.

The question is, how do I become a leader that responds versus reacts?

1.  ***It would help if you were self-aware with your emotions.***
    Self-awareness is a vital aspect of leadership and life in general. It enables you to be more introspective and ask tough questions when making decisions or facing conflicts. It also helps you evaluate challenging situations to determine whether they align with your values and standards.

    It's asking questions like:

    "Why did I feel that way when that occurred?"

    "Why did I react that way in that situation?"

    "Why did I get offended by that comment?"

    This introspection helps you understand why you operate the way you do and provides data to make necessary changes. It's less about the external factors being to blame, and more about you assessing your thoughts, emotions, and behaviors when faced with challenging moments.

2.  ***You don't need to decide on an emotional high or low.***
    As soon as I became a lead pastor, I adopted a new approach to decision-making. I give myself seventy-two hours before making an important decision. This is because it takes me at least three days to sort out my emotions and filter them out with the truth, which is the Word of God. It also gives me enough time to determine whether my decision aligns with the Word of God and my values. After seventy-two hours, I've usually run through a range of emotions such as stress, fear, anger, anxiousness, excitement, and much more. Sometimes,

it's better to let an email breathe before responding, not to answer a text immediately or to post something later. It's always wise to take your time and exercise caution.

Obviously, you're not always going to have the luxury of waiting seventy-two hours to make a sound decision, but the more you deal with conflict, tough issues, and challenging moments, and have success in the outcomes, the more confident you can become when having to make tough calls in a shorter amount of time. Unless it's life or death, there is always a window of time to be able to process.

3. ***You need to seek counsel.***
The Bible teaches that seeking counsel from multiple sources is wise. This is especially true when I have to make a tough decision. I not only pray to the Lord for guidance but also seek advice from wise people who share my faith. I am blessed to have a handful of individuals who not only possess the necessary expertise but also genuinely care about me and my success. They are not afraid to challenge me but are full of the Spirit, love the Lord, and have leadership and people management expertise.

They act as my sounding board and offer valuable insights, helping me view things from different angles I had not considered before. Their unique perspectives, shaped by their diverse experiences and roles, enrich my understanding and decision-making process.

Having a personal board for your life is essential. It's not just about having mentors or advisers, but about building a team of individuals who can hold you accountable and provide guidance when necessary. Unlike traditional mentorship or advisory relationships, a personal board is a group of people who are invested in your overall well-being and success. You should have a pastor, a leadership coach, a friend, a business leader, and a prayer partner to help you develop a well-rounded perspective. That might look different for each of you, but you need someone to help you in various facets of your life.

How do you put a personal board together? These five positions in your life, which can be catered and contoured to your industry or profession, would be beneficial. I have a person for each of these positions, and they have been game changers.

**Personal Board Positions for Your Life**
  a. Spiritual Advice (Pastor)
  b. Leadership Advice (Leadership Coach)
  c. Trusted Voice Advice (Close Friend)
  d. Skilled Person in Your Field Slightly More Ahead of You (Business Leader)
  e. Intercessor (Prayer Partner)

4. *You need to seek truth.*
When making decisions, it's best to turn to God, who has all the answers. However, we often turn to Him as a last resort when faced with obstacles. It's essential to prioritize seeking God's will first by seeking Him, His Word, and His heart for guidance. Ultimately, He has the best perspective on our situation, and His Word will illuminate our path.

This chapter aims to help you operate differently and avoid unnecessary mistakes. It's essential to remember that emails, texts, and phone calls can wait until you're in a place to make the right choice.

**Reflection Questions:**

1. As a leader, are you more prone to make emotional decisions? If so, how has that affected your leadership?
2. What changes can you begin to make in your leadership that will help you be a leader who is not reactionary but chooses to respond?
3. What steps can you take to build a personal board? Please list the names of some potential candidates below and put a plan in place to talk to them about it.
    a. Spiritual Advice _______________________________
    b. Leadership Advice _______________________________
    c. Trusted Voice Advice _______________________________
    d. Skilled Person in Your Field Slightly More Ahead of You _______________________________
    e. Intercessor _______________________________

**9**

# THE PEOPLE-PLEASING LEADER

*You can please some of the people some of the time, all of the people some of the time, some of the people all of the time, but you can never please all of the people all of the time.*
–Abraham Lincoln

*No one can make you feel inferior without your consent.*
–Eleanor Roosevelt

I can't even begin to tell you how many times my wife has encouraged me to write a book. She and many of my peers have been saying it for years. They've told me I needed to write a book on leadership because it could help so many. My response was always to thank them for the kind words yet push back on the idea. I didn't have much to say. I would also ask who would even read my book anyway. It's not like I had a massive following that would run to Amazon and purchase my book.

My pushback was rooted in my insecurities. I was more concerned about the people who wouldn't read my book than those who would. I was afraid. I was scared to put myself out there and fail. I was fearful of the opinions of others. After all, you put so much of yourself into something like a book for people to read and critique. I thought more about the critics than those who could benefit from this book. I didn't feel worthy enough to write a book. It sounds ridiculous, but it's the truth.

If you're reading this book, it's a testament to my triumph over fears and insecurities. It was a demanding journey, one that necessitated breaking through mental barriers of self-doubt and fear. I had to discover confidence in my identity and the purpose God had for me. The realization that I could have missed out on this incredible opportunity to assist others is overwhelming. Even if this book only impacts one person's life, it was all worth it.

Why was it worth it? Because I did it. I can't live with any regrets residing in the "what if" of life. That's a horrible way to live. What if I had just stepped out in faith and done that one thing that was always in my heart? In this book, you hear me talking a lot about going to the grave with unsung songs, and I firmly believe that when we look back on our lives, we should live with no regrets about what we missed out on due to our fears and insecurities.

Leadership is often accompanied by moments of fear and insecurity. The distinction between a leader and a follower is that leaders possess an innate ability to transcend their emotions of fear and insecurity to embrace the things God has for them and their communities, businesses, and families. They surpass the odds and step into victory. Victory can sometimes be disguised as failure. We also can't be naive to think that we won't ever fail when we step out, but failure is an integral part of the process and the journey as it molds us and fortifies us more than a victory ever could.

In the book *Next Generational Leader*, Andy Stanley writes a quote that has never left me based on the story of Joshua as he's getting ready to lead the Israelites into the Promised Land. He writes, "Where there is fear, there is opportunity. Where there is greater fear, there is greater opportunity." Wow! Opportunities for greatness are often clothed in scary situations. The question remains, "Will you push past your fears and insecurities to lead to the next level?"

## Let's Think About It

What would you do if you weren't afraid of what others would think of you if you did that thing? What's that one thing that's been in the back of your mind, buried deep within the crevices of your heart, that you have sensed you are supposed to do, but you've been restrained and held back by no one other than yourself and your fears and insecurities about what other people might think of you?

**WHAT WOULD YOU DO IF YOU WEREN'T AFRAID OF WHAT OTHERS WOULD THINK OF YOU IF YOU DID THAT THING?**

Some of you are reading this right now, and you have been sitting on an idea, a dream, or a vision. You're supposed to write a book, start a podcast, or pursue something you know you've been called to do, but you've been reluctant because of the fear of what others might think of you.

I'm here to let you know that doubts and fears do not come from God because he did not give you a spirit of fear or timidity but of power, love, and a sound mind. I was at this pastor's conference that I got invited to, and it was an incredible conference. One of the speakers said, within the context of leadership, that in the previous generation, pastors' biggest sin issue was pride, their pride that kept them from working together and thinking of the kingdom. It was their pride that held them back. He said, but it's no longer pride. Pride is not the biggest issue that's going to affect us today. It's our insecurities. I've realized that many of us are walking around with deep-rooted insecurities. Some of you walk and live your entire life from the framework of insecurity, wondering, if I do this, what will people think of me?

> **I'm here to let you know that doubts and fears do not come from God because he did not give you a spirit of fear or timidity but of power, love, and a sound mind.**

There is freedom when we step out in faith. But culture and society have ramped up this thing of insecurity. With social media, we have access to everyone's every move. We know everything because of your social media. We post everything. So we have

# Pride is not the biggest issue that's going to affect us today. It's our INSECURITIES

the people pleasing leader

more access to people behind the scenes, which means that we have more access to be some of the greatest critics that humanity has ever seen. Some of you have a fear of the opinions of others because you are the most opinionated person on the planet Earth. And so your project. That's an area that we must constantly work on ourselves.

You have to be careful of people-pleasing. Our insecurities often cause us to want to please those around us, so we try not to ruffle the feathers. When God calls you to something, you have two options: obey or disobey. There is no other option. Quite often, we tend to disregard because we're afraid of that one person in the congregation who has pull, that one employee who seems to have a lot of influence in the office, or that friend we're always trying to impress. If you're not careful, you could miss out on some of your life's biggest blessings and opportunities if you don't obey when God calls you to it.

## When Kings Fail

In the Bible, we come across the story of Saul, a king who provides a profound lesson on obedience to God. Saul became king at the age of thirty and ruled over Israel for forty-two years. At the beginning of his reign, Saul made a crucial decision. He selected three thousand men from Israel and sent the rest back to their homes.

Jonathan, Saul's son, attacked the Philistine outpost at Geba, and the Philistines heard about it. Saul then had the trumpet blown throughout the land and said, "Let the Hebrews hear!" So, all of Israel heard the news, and the people were summoned to join Saul at Gilgal. The Philistines gathered to fight Israel, with three thousand chariots, six thousand charioteers, and soldiers as numerous as the sand on the seashore. They camped at Mikmash, east of Beth Aven.

The Israelites found themselves in a dire situation, with their army under immense pressure. They sought refuge in caves, thickets, rocks, and pits. Some even crossed the Jordan to the land of Gad and Gilead. Meanwhile, Saul, stationed at Gilgal, was accompanied by a trembling troop. He abided by Samuel's instruction to wait for seven days, but when Samuel failed to appear, Saul's men began to scatter.

So Saul said, "Bring me the burnt offering and the fellowship offerings." And Saul offered up the burnt offering (I Samuel 13). Just as he finished making the offering, Samuel arrived, and Saul went out to greet him. Samuel asked, "What have you done?" Saul replied, "When I saw that the men were scattering and that you did not come at the set time, and that the Philistines were assembling at Mikmash, I thought, 'Now the Philistines will come down against me at Gilgal, and I have not sought the Lord's favor.' So I felt compelled to offer the burnt offering."

Samuel's words were a harsh reality check for Saul. 'You have done a foolish thing. You have not kept the command the Lord your God gave you; if you had, he would have always established your kingdom over Israel. But now your kingdom will not endure; the Lord has sought out a man after his own heart and appointed him ruler of his people because you have not kept the Lord's command.' The consequences of Saul's disobedience were severe, and this should serve as a cautionary tale for us all.

Imagine you're leading a church, a business, or a group of people when you encounter a difficult moment, and they start to abandon ship. This would make you question your leadership ability, challenge your ego, and step on your insecurities like never before.

Saul was more concerned with his image than with his standing with God. He chose to do a foolish thing in a moment of having to wait on the Lord and obey God. He offered a burnt offering, which was only meant to be done by priests or prophets. There was a sacredness to this, and Saul's action went against God's command.

Saul's disobedience stemmed from his fear of losing favor with his troops. In this, he placed the perception of people above his obedience to God, a form of idolatry. The lesson here is clear—it is far more important to seek favor with the Lord than to seek favor with people. This should instill in us a sense of urgency to prioritize our relationship with God above all else.

We can learn from Saul's mistake and stop trying to keep and please people that have exited our lives. Saul wasted his efforts on pleasing people who left, and ignored the ones who stayed. We do the same thing. It could have been God who was purging those who were truly for Him versus those who only followed Him for a status.

God will test you more when they leave than when they stay. The more you walk in obedience to God, the more the layers of toxic friendships, relationships, and people will peel off you. If you're not careful, you'll start appeasing people instead of pleasing God through your obedience.

**God will test you more when they leave than when they stay.**

If you're not careful to keep your insecurities at bay, you'll decide to please those around you instead of God.

In the Bible, Samuel referred to Saul as foolish. Foolishness did not refer to a lack of intelligence, but a lack of moral and spiritual insight. Moral and spiritual insight is only found in the realm of abiding in the Father. Pride removes us from the presence and leads us astray to follow our own will.

Am I saying God will remove you from your leadership position because you don't act on an opportunity? No! I'm trying to convey that obeying God is better than succumbing to man's thoughts.

In leadership, you will constantly be confronted with moments in which you can make tough calls and decisions. If you're not careful to keep your insecurities at bay, you'll decide to please those around you instead of God.

> **If you're not careful to keep your insecurities at bay, you'll decide to please those around you instead of God.**

There will be moments of opportunity for you that will come clothed in and wrapped in fear that you will have to lean into if you desire to see victory and results.

## People-Pleasing

What we fail to realize is that people-pleasing is a form of idolatry. You'd instead choose to look filtered rather than authentic. We don't consider this a serious issue, but it is significant. It's so big that it knocked Saul off his kingship and the generations to come from him. Idolatry is a sin, and it essentially takes God off the throne and places people's thoughts and opinions in His place. You end up serving a new master who usually enslaves you to the thoughts and opinions of people. God is a jealous God and desires that we have no idols before Him.

> **God is a jealous God and desires that we have no idols before Him.**

I think in order for us to understand the gravity of how this can negatively affect us, we have to understand the weight of the sin and view people-pleasing as a sin issue. This will hopefully bring about a new conviction within us that allows us to walk in freedom and confidence.

People-pleasing is often when you do not want to hurt people's feelings. Sometimes, People do not want to deal with a brokenness within them and would rather be liked more than anything. Because of that, we walk with a false sense of confidence when we're genuinely broken. It can often lead to surrounding yourself with people who are possibly fake and "yes" men or women to feed the fractured ego within you.

First, it's up to you to identify if this area of your life and leadership has affected you and could very well be affecting you. Second, it's essential to determine why this is an issue in your life. You can finally begin to deal with it when you can identify why it's an issue. God didn't call you to live under the weight and bondage of people-pleasing.

## How to Overcome People's Pleasing: Three Steps

*First Step*

Reconfigure your perspective. Hopefully, after reading the above, you understand the weight and gravity of what people-pleasing produces and how God views it. This should allow for an eye-opening moment within you that would realign your perspective. Remember that just because you attempt to rid yourself of concern for others' options as it pertains to your obedience and faith does not indicate that you will never wrestle with these thoughts. The more you push past them, the easier it becomes. You must also realize that leadership comes with having tough skin and a tender heart.

*Second Step*

You must also prepare yourself to receive criticism and the opinions of others but with a correct and mature heart. At the same time, you must also be ready to receive the encouragement that will come with stepping out in faith.

*Third Step*

Don't give a rip. It's not the most complex or deep thought you were possibly desiring, but it's the most upfront and true statement I live by. This does not mean that I don't ask for council or search for wisdom in decision-making and taking steps of faith, but what it does mean is that once I have the green light from the Lord, I choose not to allow the critiques of others affect my decision or confidence in my decision.

I truly live to please the Lord in all my ways, including faith and obedience to Him. When He calls you to it, He will always lead you through it.

No longer can you afford to live in fear. This is the time and the hour for you to step out and write that book, start that business, record the podcast, plant that church, and lead with confidence and the authority heaven has granted you.

## Reflection Questions

1. What fears and insecurities have prevented you from pursuing something you truly desire?
2. What would you do if you weren't afraid of what others would think of you if you pursued that thing?
3. How can you overcome your fears and insecurities and step out in faith? What steps can you take to push past your fears and pursue your goals and dreams?
4. How can you cultivate confidence and resilience in the face of fear and insecurity?
5. How can you shift your mindset from focusing on the opinions of others to concentrate on your purpose and calling?

10

# LIVING THE DREAM

*The four Cs of making dreams come true: Curiosity, Courage,
Consistency, Confidence.*
–Walt Disney

*Dreams require down payments. Dreams are free, but the journey
isn't. There is a price to pay. When you find your why you'll find
your way. When you develop your will you will embark on your
way. Many people start; few people finish. Many people have a
dream; few people achieve their dreams.*
–John C. Maxwell

From the depths of my memory, I recall a time when my response to the question "How are you?" was always, "Living the dream." Yet, the truth was far from it. My words were laced with sarcasm, a shield to hide the reality that I was barely holding on, my dreams seemingly out of reach.

Honestly, I felt like I would never reach a place in my ministry life where I would feel as though I were living the dream. Life in ministry had beat me down for so many years. Yet, despite all the challenges, I persisted. I felt that all of the wins and whatever success I had wasn't enough to outweigh the hard seasons that never seemed to end—working for the wrong people and feeling like I was giving my life to leaders and places that would only crush me in the end and make me feel as if though it was my fault. If you've ever been caught in the ocean where the waves come in at frequent intervals with little time between each break—yeah, that's what leadership and ministry felt like for so long.

Ministry is hard, but when the people you're supposed to look up to make it even harder, it tends to make no sense. I felt like I was dragged through the mud more than once, and all hope of there ever being a light at the end of the tunnel was almost completely gone. The light that once shone so bright was but a faint flicker at best that could at any moment be put out with a simple slight of breath.

With so many questions but not enough answers and with so much skepticism for the future, this was my lot in life and ministry.

That I would always be in these situations and that any hopes I had of finding a place to be me, spread my wings, and soar was a frivolous dream that only happened to everyone else but me.

## God Was in It

Little did I know that God was moving in it all. There was not a time that He wasn't moving. You see, I had thought that the process from where I stood to fulfilling the vision for my life and ministry would be a straight shot. I never anticipated that the road would be so winding, filled with moments in which I would take five steps forward and yet another three steps back. I never factored that for every mountaintop moment; more valleys lay ahead. I hadn't considered every experience pleasant, and some would bring much disappointment and pain.

Looking back from the moment I graduated from Bible School to the present, I've come to a profound realization. It's a truth I've always known in theory, but now I know it in my bones. God was not just present in my journey; He was orchestrating it. Every step, every setback, every victory was part of His plan. Not a second of that time was wasted, for God was leading me through the valleys, just as the Holy Spirit led Jesus into the wilderness. He was working everything out for my good, and I had to trust in His timing and His promises.

God will give you the vision and then lead you through the valley of humility to work it out in you so that He can work it out through you. He's obviously more concerned with who you're becoming along the journey than with your arrival at your destination.

# THE DREAM

GOD WILL GIVE YOU THE VISION
AND THEN LEAD YOU THROUGH THE
VALLEY OF HUMILITY TO WORK IT
OUT IN YOU SO THAT HE CAN
WORK IT OUT THROUGH YOU.

# LIVING

## When God Promises

God promised Abraham and Sarah that they would have a son, Isaac. This would be impossible in the natural because Sarah was well past her child-bearing years. It could only happen through a miracle. Very understandably, they both didn't really believe that it would really happen. From the moment that God gave them that promise until its fulfillment, it took twenty-five years.

It's easy to understand how they could have gotten weary after so many years of seeing no results. I can only imagine their first conversations about what they would name the child and who the child would mostly look like. I wonder if they began preparing a room in their home in anticipation of the arrival of this promised child. Only to find themselves in a place of waiting and waiting and waiting. I'm sure that discouragement kicked in. I'm sure that anger and frustration arose within them. I wonder if there was ever tension between them.

After twelve years of waiting, Sarah finally had it. She was at her wit's end and decided that Abraham should lie with her maidservant and help God in the process. I wonder if she felt the need to help God in this way because maybe He was so busy being God that He had forgotten about them and His promise.

As the story goes, Abraham lies with Hagaar, and she becomes pregnant and gives birth to Ishmael. As we know, that didn't turn out well for either party involved. In the end, Haggar was sent away, and just thirteen years later, Sarah became pregnant and bore a son named Issac, the promised child.

In her disappointment and despair, Sarah was willing to settle for what was good instead of waiting for God's best. She and

Abraham attempted to make something happen, failing to realize that God was at work within those twenty-five years. God was setting the stage for the main event. He was preparing things at the right time. He had never stopped working. He was never going to negate His promise. He was also not going to speed up the process for the promise. He was going to deliver in His timing, and His timing is always perfect. This is a reminder to all of us that patience is a virtue, and waiting for God's timing is always worth it.

We must understand that God has a promise for all of us. He has a plan to prosper you and not to harm you, to give you hope and a future. He has a promise with your name on it. It also includes a time stamp. There is a vacuum of space from the declaration of His promises to their fulfillment. The time in between is called the process, which is always challenging. It's not for the faint of heart. Being a leader doesn't come like furniture in a showroom where it's assembled. It's more like IKEA furniture that comes in 157,000 pieces and takes time to understand and build.

What has God promised you that you've yet to see come to pass? Have, you've grown wearing in doing good? Scriptures declare that in the proper time, we'll reap a harvest if we don't give up. That promise in Galatians 6:9 is conditional, which means that it is yours under the condition given within it. The condition is that you can't give up. If you don't, the promise is yours.

Maybe you've thought about throwing in the towel, or perhaps you have. If that's you, then maybe this is the moment in which God desires to throw it back and say it's not over. Why? Because He's still moving. He hasn't stopped moving. He's been setting your stage for the right time, His time. Don't settle for what's good when what's best is around the corner. Don't settle for a partial promise when His heart is to give you the whole package.

## Don't settle for what's good when what's best is around the corner.

### Living The Dream

I never thought I would live the dream, but I am. It's not because I have a mega ministry with hundreds and thousands of social media followers or because I'm traveling the world speaking at conferences. I've had the opportunity to do that, which brought me no joy. It was more like a drug that required more and more to feel good for a moment.

I'm living the dream because, for the first time in my ministry life and leadership, I understand why my journey was so challenging. I know why there were so many valley moments. I can finally see why I had to go through such hardship. It was because those moments served as the hammer and chisel that carved away the excess clay to form me more into His image. They were the very moments He used to forge in me a grit like no other to steady the course. They were the intended moments that God used to bring me to the simplicity of the Gospel—learning to love God and love people the way He does.

It's been an eye-opening experience pastoring a newly established church for the past two and a half years. Witnessing the transformation and growth within such a short time has been nothing short of remarkable. Reflecting on the past, I can see how every tough season has contributed to my evolution as a leader, and I am eager to continue learning and growing in my role.

Leading this extraordinary church has been a privilege, and we have been deliberate in setting the culture and direction based on our collective past experiences. It's truly rewarding to see how our past has served as a guide, helping us determine what practices to embrace and which ones to discard.

Reflecting on my journey, it's remarkable to think that I could have missed out on all of this if I had given up during moments of doubt instead of persevering and pushing through.

The greatest joy of my life is being a husband to my incredible wife and a father to my four amazing children. The process I went through was not to become a great leader in the church, but to be the best version of myself for me and for my family. Your journey will never be a straight line that instantly leads to your goal. It will be different for each person, and it will be challenging. Learn to embrace the difficult times as much as you do the good times because something is happening in and through it all. You won't be able to see it all right now. It's like a puzzle with 1,000 pieces constantly being put together. You won't be able to see the whole picture with just a few assembled pieces. It's not until each piece is perfectly fitted where it needs to be that the picture becomes clear.

One day, you'll be able to look back and see why the journey took the turns that it did, why you took the paths that you did, and why it seemed like God decided to take you the long way around to get to your promise when He could have cut corners and got you there in fourteen days. Who you're becoming is far more important than where you're going.

You've got this! You might not be where you want to be but thank God you're no longer the person you used to be. You're being molded to be more and more like Him. Don't give up, ever! The time is now, so don't waste it!

In your corner,
Alberto Bello

**Reflection Questions:**

1.  How do you relate to the author's experience of feeling beaten down and discouraged in their ministry or personal life?
2.  Have you ever felt the need to "help" God make something happen because you thought He was taking too long?
3.  What promises or dreams do you feel impatient about or might be tempted to take control of instead of waiting for God's timing?
4.  How do you think the "living the dream" concept applies to your life? Do you feel like you are living your dream, or are there challenges and obstacles you must overcome to get there?
5.  What are some ways you have seen God working in your life, even during challenging or discouraging times?

# ABOUT THE AUTHOR

Alberto, a visionary from the start, is known for his passion, drive, and relevance. His unique ability to connect with individuals and inspire them to know God, love God, and love people has been instrumental in helping them maximize their fullest potential here on earth.

After rededicating his life to Christ at the age of 22 at Teen Challenge, he answered the call to ministry. He and his wife, Ashley, spent their early years in South Central LA and Bakersfield as Youth Pastor's while serving as student advisors at the Teen Challenge Ministry Institute.

In 2013, Pastor Alberto and Ashley established The Gathering LA, a church that left a significant mark in the heart of Los Angeles. Their influence was so profound that they were offered a TV Show on the TBN Salsa Network, titled 'Life in the City.' Pastor Alberto's leadership extended beyond the church, as he served as the lead campus pastor for New Season, overseeing all of their existing campuses. He also made a substantial contribution to the NHCLC, (National Hispanic Christian Leadership Conference) as their marketing director. After a fruitful time in Sacramento, they returned to Bakersfield, this time as Associate Pastors at

Bakersfield First Assembly of God, the same church where they once served as Youth Pastors.

Today, Pastor Alberto and his wife Ashley are at the helm of a new church plant, The Collective. This vibrant community is a shining example of hope and growth, situated in the heart of Bakersfield, California. The Collective, under their leadership, is committed to fostering a welcoming and loving environment, where individuals can grow in their faith and make a positive impact in the city. It stands as a testament to their vision and leadership, a young, thriving, and growing church situated in the heart of Downtown.

Alberto and Ashley, a testament to unwavering dedication, have been married for 16 years and have 4 children: Brooklyn, Talia, Mateo, and Milo. Their family is a living example of the power of faith and the strength it brings to relationships.